Further Views from the Floor

Hugh B. Black

with

Dr Alison H. Black

New Wine Press

New Wine Press
PO Box 17
Chichester PO20 6YB
England

Unless otherwise stated, all biblical references are taken from the
Authorised Version. Also used: NIV – The Holy Bible, New
International Version. Copyright © 1973, 1978, 1984 New York Bible
Society. Published by Hodder and Stoughton.

ISBN: 1 874367 72 8

Other books by Hugh Black

The Baptism in the Spirit and Its Effects
Reflections on the Gifts of the Spirit
Reflections on a Song of Love (1 Corinthians 13)
A Trumpet Call to Women
The Clash of Tongues: With Glimpses of Revival
Consider Him (Twelve Qualities of Christ)
Battle for the Body
The Incomparable Christ
Gospel Vignettes
Reflections from Abraham
Reflections from Moses: With the Testimony of Dan McVicar
Christ the Deliverer
Christian Fundamentals
Reflections from David
Pioneers of the Spiritual Way
Revival: Including the Prophetic Vision of Jean Darnall
Revival: Personal Encounters
Revival: Living in the Realities
War in Heaven and Earth
A View from the Floor
E.H. Taylor: A Modern Christian Mystic (edited by Hugh Black)

Typeset by CRB Associates, Reepham, Norfolk
Printed in England by Clays Ltd, St Ives plc.

Dedication

To all saints who realize that
'broken we conquer'

Contents

Foreword

This book is the second in a series in which the author draws together experiences of Christians from many different backgrounds, who have found their lives enriched by what has come to be known as 'the new ministry'. As you read the reports you will be struck by the wide diversity of circumstance which prompted the people to reach out to God in this new and, to some reserved Scottish temperaments, very public way. However, one common factor pervades each of the stories – every life regardless of intellectual background, social status or spiritual maturity has had an encounter with the Divine.

Some relatively young Christians report that the experience of coming to God's operating table has transformed their lives. Other testimonies come from lives whose service of Christ has spanned decades and whose devotion to Him and His flock is above reproach. Yet for them also there has come a new revelation of God through their beloved Christ by the power of the Holy Spirit.

For me, the atmosphere of these experiences is effectively conveyed in one of the songs written in the early days of the new flow:

> There's a road that is open before us
> And it leads to a world unknown ...[1]

The road is still open, and as you read the book it is my prayer that you will find your heart strangely warmed with a desire to take that step of faith that will lead you into a new place of richness in your Christian life.

Irene Morrison

Note

[1] See chapter 2.

Preface

Towards the end of 1994 there came to the Struthers Memorial group of churches a movement of the Spirit of God that has continued to the present day. Beginning at our conference in High Wycombe in the south of England, it quickly spread to our churches north of the border. Testimonies to its effectiveness were abundant; many of these were recorded on tape and so could be drawn on for publication. The first group chosen appeared in *A View from the Floor*; it was by then evident that what had been planned as a single volume was turning into a series, of which this is the second volume.

All these books range widely over a variety of experiences. But whereas the first dwells on the origins of the 'new ministry' through which many went prostrate under the power of the Holy Spirit, the second examines in some detail the ways in which new avenues of worship and access to God were opened up. The third, while continuing to explore the abundance of the land we are entering, links testimonies with themes such as the breaking down of walls of prejudice, the Christian scene both Scottish and worldwide, and the question of revival.

I wish to thank those who have allowed me to use their testimonies and other spoken or written contributions. To my wife Isobel and to Jennifer Jack for their helpful suggestions and proofreading labours, I am particularly grateful. Finally, a word about authorship. My daughter Dr Alison Black, an academic author and editor in her own right, has had an increasingly significant role in the shaping of this series. For this reason her name appears here as co-author, although first-person references in the main text are to myself.

Hugh B. Black

Chapter 1

A Healing Fragrance

The phone had rung when I was out. I called back early that evening, to discover one of our congregation in severe distress. It was **Mary M**, an ambulance driver; but on this occasion it was not in handling patients that her problem had arisen. With an engaging mixture of humour and honesty she tells her story:

It was pure disobedience. That's the only way I can describe how I hurt my back. I had been told earlier that day to leave the job till the weekend. But in my younger days in the church I had been taught, 'If there's a job to be done go and do it: don't wait for other people.' And so I looked at the big pile of curtains on my sitting room floor. They were velvet, they were newly made, and they had to be fitted in our Gourock church.

The minister, Mr Cleary, had just departed, saying, 'Leave that job. That's for Saturday.'

I said, 'Right.'

And he wasn't long away when I piled all the curtains into the car and went down to the church.

Now before all this happened I had had a strange feeling to go to our Saturday night meeting in Glasgow. To do so meant replacing my eight-hour shift in the ambulance services by a sixteen-hour shift

extending from Friday afternoon to Saturday morning
and taking in one of the two busiest nights of the week.

But today was Thursday, and I was getting on fine
hooking up the curtains with the help of the big
ladders – except for the curtain at each end of the
platform. One went up with a struggle. The other
proved recalcitrant, but eventually the last hook
went in.

Coming back down I missed a step and fell backwards, hitting the platform, and landing somewhere
down by the piano.

Hurt in the base of my spine, I lay there pondering
which was worse – the sixteen-hour shift ahead or the
lecture I was going to get from Mr Cleary. Neither
prospect attracted. The immediate problem was how
to get off the floor, since no one else would be in the
building before Saturday. Thinking, 'I'll have to get
out of here,' I crawled to the back of the church,
pulled myself upright and got myself sufficiently
mobile to lock up the church and drive home.

'I should really stop at Mr Cleary's,' I thought.
Outside his door I hesitated: 'Will I? ... won't I?' I
knew what the consequences would be!

But he was not in.

He was still not in when I phoned from home a
while later. Nor was Mr Black available when I tried
to contact him.

The pain was excruciating, and I was worried about
the ambulance shift, for my absence would have
meant the driver coping single-handed. The only
position in which I could get any relief was on my
knees: I stayed in that position.

At quarter to six the phone rang.

'Let me get an ambulance for you,' suggested
Mr Black.

'No, no! I have always sworn that if they ever have
to come to my door I'll crawl out, because I'll never
let them lift me!'

So Mr Black prayed over the phone and promised to phone back in an hour. But an hour later there was no change in my condition. I was still in agony.

Less than half an hour had passed after his second phone call when the doorbell rang, and in came both Mr Black and Mr Cleary.

'This is it!' I thought.

But something unexpected was in store for Mary. During the previous few months, since November 1994, a new ministry had been operating in the church, a particular anointing that very often caused the recipient to go prostrate under the direct ministry of the Holy Spirit.[1] Mary had not previously sought this, nor was she seeking it now. Yet as she came in her physical need and we prayed with her, God gave more than she had asked or thought.

She was kneeling at her chair in agony. Suddenly it was like a bolt from the blue, and she stretched out right on her back on the floor. To say I actually heard a crack would be overstating it, but there was a feeling of something happening. All pain died out of her body. She ultimately sat up and said, 'The pain has gone!'

Describing the experience afterwards, she said:

> The only thing that I can remember of the time of prayer is the beautiful fragrance that filled the room. I went down before the Lord; He just filled and filled and filled my life. The overpowering fragrance of Christ stayed there all night. In the morning when I came into the room it was still there.
>
> And the pain was gone.

But, she added,

> the lecture was still to come. Mr Cleary doesn't give up lightly! I endured it. And I did my sixteen-hour shift, and I told my story at the Saturday night

13

meeting. Praise the Lord for what He has done in my body and in my life![2]

Far beyond the physical healing of her back was the sense of the invading fragrance of Christ that affected Mary's inner being. A similar experience befell another lady about a month later, this time just where she sat in one of our services. The atmosphere in a gathering where God was moving could be such that spontaneous miracles occurred without any ministry being sought. **Pat** was a visitor to our Easter conference in 1995. Her story is told by the lady who brought her, Effie Alexander, leader of our Edinburgh fellowship.

'How did you get on?' I asked.

It had been a lovely meeting, in which God was very present. But my friend Pat, a convert of less than a year's standing, had never attended such a large gathering before, and it was her first visit to Greenock.

'Phhhewww!' Pat has a very expressive way of putting things. 'That was heavy!'

But it wasn't heavy in the oppressive sense: there was just the weight of God's presence.

'That smell,' she continued, 'it was beautiful! I've never smelt anything like that before!'

I wouldn't like to say I was jealous! But I was absolutely delighted for her, as she kept saying, 'Oh, it was beautiful; it was just beautiful.'

The Lord had spoken to her and said, 'Pat, reach out your hand.'

Prior to that she had been nursing her arm, which was very painful with arthritis. Obediently she reached out her hand, and as she did so, she was healed! In the words of the hymn:

> His garments too were in cassia dipped,
> With healing in a touch ...[3]

Later she confirmed that the pain was all gone – and provided us with a demonstration. But you felt that her overwhelming consciousness was of the presence of the Lord and of that beautiful fragrance that had touched her spirit.

There had been many healings in our midst long before the dawn of the new ministry. They had sometimes occurred spontaneously, and often they had come clothed with a sense of the fragrance of Christ. Even in the years that have followed, not every healing has been associated with the new ministry or borne the mark of that specific anointing and atmosphere. But it certainly was increasingly the case that when people came with requests for prayer of various kinds, God met them in this new way. And in many cases, it was not until He met them in this way that they found the answer to their needs.

An instructive example is the case of **Richard**, a student in teacher-training. Before the advent of the new ministry, he had sought prayer for healing:

When neuralgia first affected me I became conscious of a trembling feeling on the side of my head. It was often there, and it began to get quite sore. It then started to travel from my head down to my tooth; it tingled there as well as in my head and became really painful. That went on for months. At one point I went to Mr Black and asked him to pray with me. The trembling stopped, but the pain got worse and actually started to spread down my neck and then down my shoulder to my arm. It was there day and night, especially in circumstances of stress. When I had a lot of studying to do, I'd experience pain and tension all the time.

Six months later the problem had still not cleared. But

by this time, mid-January 1995, God had been moving through the new ministry for the past two months, and Richard was to receive his portion.

About two weeks ago on the Friday night the pain was very bad. It had been troubling me all day, and when I woke up on the Saturday morning it was still there. Throughout the day I felt that I was to go for prayer that night. I wasn't too keen on that idea! I didn't really want to go forward. (I had gone forward before and had felt quite confused.) But as I sat in my seat and felt the drawing of God to get up, I did so: in cold blood I stood up in the aisle and switched off my mind from worrying, and went through to God. It was really very easy just to switch off and worship God.

Mr Black passed by and touched my head very lightly, and I went down. It was like lying on a beach with the waves coming up and down; it was very lovely. I felt so much at peace, so relaxed. I hadn't felt relaxed in over a year. I tried to get up at one point and couldn't. A few minutes passed by and then I did get up, and when I sat down somebody else fell down where I had been!

Back in my seat I felt everything so wonderfully loose. Neuralgia is very painful, like having toothache all over one side of your body: it's always there. But now I felt as if somebody had untied something down one side and all was right again. I thought, 'You've done it! You've healed me; You've taken it away.' Having had it for a year, I sat now and drank it in.

The next day at college I felt great, and was able to cope with an amount of work that would normally have made me really stressed and tense. I thought, 'O God, You've healed me!' What He had done was just beginning to sink in. I kept meeting my Christian friends and saying, 'Guess what happened to me!' I told them because I had been moaning to them so often, 'Oh, my head's really sore,' and I think they were probably getting a bit sick of it. But now it was totally gone, and every time I spoke to somebody about it I could feel that same presence of God that was there during the experience. I met umpteen people throughout the next week or two!

What God has done is amazing. It's like not having an arm and then having it again. And I praise Him for it.

One of the wonderful things about this new movement was to see God Himself in action. This story of Richard's thrilled my heart. There he lay on the operating table of God; man didn't get in the road in any way, and the living God Himself directly healed him.

There was one of our members, **Agnes**, who, like Richard, was at first exceedingly unwilling to go on to that operating table.[4] And yet if she had not overcome her fear she would have found herself in a human operating theatre for a condition she had some reason to dread. Agnes tells her own story:

For two or three weeks my health had been failing pretty badly, and I had felt myself going down low spiritually. Despite the encouragement of our Port Glasgow minister, Joan Jewell, to ask for prayer, my reaction was, 'You're not getting me down on that floor – no way!' I felt unusually shy and embarrassed.

'You don't know what happens, you know!' said Joan.

'I just don't care!' I was insistent I wasn't going on that floor.

But one Sunday morning God moved in Port Glasgow in the same way as in Greenock. I don't know why, but it just broke me. As my two daughters stood for ministry, I thought, 'Lord, look at my two

17

daughters, and their mother can't even stand up!'
Then Joan came over to me, and out I went.

In all truthfulness I don't know what God did to
me when I was lying on the floor. But the next day I
was telling Joan that I was awaiting an operation for
a fairly large lump. The idea of a lump always
brought on me the fear of cancer, because my sister
had died of cancer starting from a lump.

Joan encouraged Agnes to approach me. Her initial
experience 'on the carpet' had broken the ice of her
resistance to the new ministry, and so she came to see me
in our church bookshop, scene of many an eventful
encounter! On this occasion we went through into the
church, where we prayed very simply, and down she went.
I spoke for a little time and left her lying there.

I give you warning: if you ever come into our church
some day unexpectedly and there's somebody lying there,
don't worry about it, because I tend to leave them
there! They come to in due time; at least they always have
done so up till now!

Agnes describes what happened to her:

Again I went down in the Spirit and lay prostrate. I
was aware of God and the peace within me. By
Wednesday the lump had shrunk to about the size of
a postage stamp. By Thursday, the lump had disappeared completely. My appetite, which is normally
healthy, had left me for about two weeks, and I had
just been nibbling: now I couldn't stop eating! I give
God all the praise and glory for what He's done.

Needless to say, Agnes's next visit to the hospital
confirmed that there was no lump. It is wonderful to let
God operate. I can't heal people of lumps. The glory
is God's.

✢ ✢ ✢

Physical healing was only one aspect of what awaited many who lay on God's operating table. It may not have been the most important aspect; but for the reader it serves as an outward, communicable evidence for the reality of the Spirit's moving. The ensuing chapters provide first-hand accounts of a wide range of experiences that demonstrated God's care for the whole being, physical, mental and spiritual. He did not merely come down to where we were: He took us into a realm where He made Himself known in a new way, and where miracles seemed to happen naturally and spontaneously.

The joy with which His coming infected our spirits is expressed in one of the songs which I wrote at this time. Entitled 'Early Rains', for us it was a real departure from tradition! [5]

> There'll be laughing, laughing, laughing
>   On the floors of earth
> As God's chosen people
>   Come to second birth.
>
> There'll be weeping, weeping, weeping
>   As the waters break,
> As a generation's
>   Old foundations shake.
>
> There'll be singing, singing, singing
>   Tuning into glory,
> With a holy nation
>   Sounding out the story.
>
> There'll be dancing, dancing, dancing
>   There before the throne
> As a joyous people
>   Worship God alone.
>
> Laughing, weeping, singing, dancing,
>   See the hosts of God advancing,
> See the powers of darkness yield
>   As Judah's lion takes the field.

Laughing, weeping, dancing, singing,
  Hear the courts of heaven ringing;
This the long-awaited hour,
  This the day of heaven's power.

Rivers rising, strong tides swelling,
  Feel the waters fast upwelling;
This the coming glorious flood,
  A church triumphant through the blood.

One or other of these themes – weeping, laughing, singing and dancing – was prominent in many testimonies. There were others, however, whose experience on the floor was of an entirely different order. The chapters that follow indicate something of the variety of the Holy Spirit's dealings with individual lives.

Notes

[1] The story of how this new ministry began and how it affected many lives is told in the first volume of this series, *A View from the Floor* (New Wine Press, 1997). Like this present book, the first is based largely on testimonies.

[2] The story of Mary's earlier healing from an unusual phobia, stemming from an attack by a bird, is told in my book *Christ the Deliverer* (New Dawn Books, 1991). More recently, through an unpleasant experience in an elevator, she found herself panicking when locked into a prison cell in the course of her routine work with the ambulance service. She came for prayer and was immediately set free. On both occasions she tested the reality of her healing by going back into the situations which had caused the fear. Whether it was of birds or of prison cells – it had truly gone.

[3] Quoted from the hymn 'Ivory Palaces'.

[4] Agnes appears in one of my earlier books along with her daughter Kirsty. The story of their instantaneous healing is told there by Joan Jewell, who had prayed with them. See *Revival: Living in the Realities* (New Dawn Books, 1993), chapter 9.

[5] For an account of how I came to write what turned out to be the first of a series of new hymns ('The Song of Jesus'), see *A View from the Floor*, chapter 3.

Chapter 2

Laughter – in Church?

'Laughing ... in church?'

When not only the one lying on the floor but the minister herself was overcome by gales of laughter, people might well wonder. But for **Gillian**, there was no perplexity – only a joyous surprise that turned sorrow into gladness of heart and transformed her life as a probationer teacher.

Gillian had already known a marvellous touch of God in healing when she had gone down under ministry nearly three months previously, towards the end of November 1994. Her experience on that occasion is worth recounting, not only for the sake of the miracle, but also because it had helped to open up her life more fully to God than ever before.

Like many others, she did not immediately perceive the relevance of the new moving of God to her own life:

> When the new ministry first came to the church I felt I was quite open to it, having witnessed similar prostrations in a fellowship I had previously attended. At the same time, I didn't think that it was for me. (How many people have said that?)

Gillian was to learn otherwise. What brought her to the front for ministry a week later was a problem with her health. It had started at one of our church camps:

At the August camp, along with all the toddlers in the Falkirk church, I managed to catch chickenpox. After being quite unwell with it for two or three weeks I went back to work feeling as though I hadn't really recovered. I was tired constantly, and this got progressively worse until I was forced to go to the doctor about three months later. He said that I had a post-viral infection, and the implication of that was a constant weariness. I couldn't concentrate on anything for any length of time; all I could do was go to my work, come home and go to bed. And that was about as exciting as life got! I certainly didn't manage to go to church – including Saturday nights in Greenock, for I couldn't face the journey.

Life didn't seem to be getting any better, until last Friday at my work I recognized something which quite surprised me: I was getting annoyed and irritated at things that wouldn't normally have bothered me, and just wasn't coping with how I was feeling. When I went home I told my mum, who said, 'Have you thought about going for ministry?' I was quite shocked, because although I had seen miraculous healing in our own family, it's a different case when it's yourself, and you have to decide if you want that to happen for you! I believed that God could heal me ... I decided to go to the Glasgow outreach meeting on Friday night and ask Him either to heal me or to give me the strength to cope.

The occasion of the outreach was the first time I had been out in the evening for about a month, and I yawned my head off the whole way through the service! It was hard to keep my eyes open. Then it came to the time for ministry. Like someone else who had been determined to go forward that same night but sat in her seat when the first invitation was given,[1] I said to myself, 'Well, if Mr Black gives another invitation I'll know, Lord, that that's from You.' And sure enough, he said, 'Come for ministry.'

I got up from my seat and went to the front. Mr Black came and prayed with me, and he placed his hand very, very gently on my forehead. Almost immediately, as he spoke the words, 'The anointing of God,' there was the same sense that I associate with my baptism in the Spirit, the anointing of God just coming on me, and I felt as though I was falling into the arms of Jesus. I went into a place of complete relaxation that I hadn't experienced for many months. All the time that I had been really tired and in bed, I had never felt relaxed.

Lying on that carpet in the Glasgow church I was so relaxed that I felt as though I could have stayed there the whole night! During that time God gave my body and my mind the rest that I couldn't find physically. He touched me and in a moment of time gave me the rest that my body had been craving. There had been a heavy net, or blanket, of weariness all round my mind so that I couldn't concentrate for any length of time. As I rose from the carpet, I felt as though the net had been completely taken away. With a thrill of surprise, I thought, 'I haven't felt like this since August.' I tried to tell Mr Black, but wasn't very coherent.

When I went to bed on Friday night I couldn't tell at that point if physically I was any better, but I certainly felt that the heaviness and the blackness that was almost like a depression had been lifted and was gone. I had the best night's sleep I had had in months. When I got up at half-past seven the next morning, I was totally refreshed! I felt as if like the psalmist I could 'run through a troop, and leap over a wall'! We went shopping the whole day, and that proved I was feeling better.

Then a strange thing happened. I was getting ready to travel through to the Saturday night meeting and was looking forward to it because I hadn't been to Greenock for such a long time. Just as we were having our meal, I began to feel terribly unwell. Dizziness and nausea – all the same symptoms, including the heaviness – were coming back on me. A doubt got into my mind that I wasn't really healed at all ... or maybe God had only done it in part and had only managed to touch me slightly.

I was on the verge of staying in and going to bed, when I thought, 'Oh, no, not back into this same old pattern.' There was a voice in my head saying, 'Was your God not able to heal you?' It was as though the enemy was trying to place doubt in my mind that God wasn't able. And I knew that wasn't true. I got ready and came down in the car, feeling rotten the whole way. And as soon as I got through the door of the church, the sense of illness lifted! I felt that it was something I'd had to fight through, and that when I got here, God said to me, 'You've been faithful, and I have healed you totally.'

Since then it seems as if in this one week I have managed to fit in a whole month of what I was able to do before! There has been so much energy. I've been feeling hundreds of times better, and the miracle is that what would normally have taken months of rest and vitamin courses and balanced diet and so on, God did so quickly. In the past week the song 'Like a bird out of the nest, we have broken free,' has had such a new meaning for me. God took that net that was round about my mind and body, and totally broke it. Praise His Name!

That particular healing remained. Then in the New Year a new set of circumstances came into Gillian's life, and again it took a divine visitation to lift her to a place of victory in the midst of them. This time there were fewer reservations to overcome. She continues:

Through my healing God opened up a whole new aspect of my spiritual life. An area that had been kept firmly to myself was now open to God, and He was able to do far more in my life.

About two months ago I started a new job as a secondary school teacher. For some reason the staff were incredibly unfriendly to me! And the children! I had never met children so insolent and rude – their behaviour was awful! Having been much happier in my previous situation, I couldn't cope with the difference between the two schools. There was one class in particular that I had first thing in the morning for three double periods a week: by the time they left the room I was nearly in tears, drained and worn out and ready to pack it all in.

By the end of three weeks I was thinking about what Jennifer Rees Larcombe had said during her visit to us about her 'peace-joy'. I felt that my peace-joy had been completely taken away. It wasn't that I had lost it through carelessness, but that it had been worn down by the events of the weeks. By the time it got to a week past on Sunday I was really down, feeling that I was a failure and shouldn't be in teaching – and worse still, that as a Christian I should be able to cope with a difficult job situation, and that I was letting God down by how I was feeling. So it was a vicious circle where I felt that I wasn't coping and I should be coping, hence I was a failure – which made me feel even more of a failure. I cried non-stop the whole of that day, until it was time for the evening service.

The theme of the sermon that night was God's promise to repay the years that the locusts had eaten. The speaker, Gillian's mother, applied it to Naomi in the book of Judges, but to Gillian the past two months of her own life had no doubt seemed like years:

Feeling the theme very appropriate to my situation, I went forward for ministry. As Jennifer (Jack) prayed with me I felt all my sorrow drain away.[2] And then something really amazing happened. I was hit with a tidal wave of laughter! I went down on the floor and lay there and laughed and laughed and laughed! As that blanket of laughter was over me, all the hurts and anxiety and irritation and feelings of failure totally drained away.

In the last couple of weeks since that happened, the situation at school has not changed very much, but God has changed me in it. I have that peace and laughter with me all the time – especially when this class goes away! It's as though I can just turn to God and feel all that bubbling up inside me again – and I certainly never thought I would be laughing in this situation. But I praise God for what He has done; it is amazing that He can move in such a way and meet such sorrow with such joy. Praise Him!

We naturally rejoiced with Gillian as we heard her testimony. Some of us had known holy laughter in our own experience through the years. There were many, however, for whom it was a new and strange phenomenon, and it was not surprising that some of those listening to such laughter wondered at the time what it was all about.

Sensing disturbance amongst some of our members, **Jennifer Jack** offered useful comment initially to her own church in Falkirk and then to the larger company that met in Greenock on a Saturday night. She had been studying Dr Patrick Dixon's book *Signs of Revival*, but when invited to read the relevant portion aloud for the benefit of the Greenock congregation, she laughingly declined, for a reason that will become apparent later:

A week after Gillian's experience, as I sat at home wondering what God wanted for the approaching

26

service that Sunday evening, I picked up Patrick Dixon's *Signs of Revival*.[3] Near the beginning of the book there was the testimony of a man who was affected by laughter quite against his will. As I started to read it I started to laugh and couldn't stop laughing! Eventually I went on and read a bit more, and began to think a bit more about the meeting, and came back and read the passage several times; and every time I read it I was laughing – not just smiling, but actually laughing out loud as I was reading it. Of course it brought back to me what had happened to Gillian the week before, when there had come that wave of laughter which had swept over her and myself at the same time. I thought we would have Gillian's testimony to that in the meeting, prefaced by the extract from the book. And then I thought I couldn't possibly read the extract!

So I left the book at home and told the company what I knew of the therapeutic effect of laughter in the natural sphere. I can remember a situation in a school staff room where someone was telling a story, and while we weren't actually rolling on the floor we were doubled up with laughter so that we couldn't talk – the person telling the story couldn't finish it. After it was all over I remember saying, 'I feel so much better after that,' and everybody else agreed. There was a sense of healing inside and a release of tension. And if that happens in the natural, how much more in the spiritual?

I then explained why I had not brought the book I had been reading, but proceeded to tell them what it said ... only I couldn't tell them, because I kept on bursting into fits of laughter! It was very embarrassing indeed! I kept on turning away from the company and trying to get a grip of myself just as the man in the story tries to do, and I could feel little ripples of laughter coming from one part of the company, and then they would get a grip of themselves and it would start over in another part. It was very, very funny. When Gillian gave her testimony she managed to control herself much better than I had!

From the feedback that came at the end of that meeting, it seems that the explanation combined with Gillian's account helped to clarify in many people's minds what it was that God was doing. Some people had previously, I think, been a bit startled or taken aback – you know, what's all this, outbursts of laughter in the church? There was a certain amount of questioning and puzzlement. Now a number found that it suddenly all made sense to them as they began to realize what God could do. What I was very conscious of with Gillian was that in 'one divine moment' God healed that situation totally and completely as hours of counselling and human intervention could never have done, and with the healing came laughter.

The irony was that when I went back to the book after the evening service, it produced nothing but a quiet smile. I have returned to it a couple of times since and it didn't seem very funny; I actually wondered if it was just the wording of the episode that had made me laugh. But what I really think happened is that something of the spirit of it touched me, and was meant to touch me, before that Sunday evening service.

I don't know that it would touch me again tonight – and that's why I'm not reading it!

A great deal of humour is related to the personality of the individual concerned, and the one featured in Dixon's book appears to be a very upright, respectable member of the community. This makes the story genuinely amusing, but it does not sufficiently account for Jennifer's reaction. One of the most sane, balanced people I have ever known, she has a wonderful sense of humour allied to an equally strong sense of normality. She is widely respected in her professional capacity as a secondary school teacher in senior management. Neither she nor any of the others whose testimonies are included in this chapter could by any stretch of imagination be said to be 'hysterical types'.

Particularly illuminating is the testimony of Gillian's mother **Kathleen**, who shared some of the misgivings of those upset by outbursts of laughter in church. Her disquiet, however, was occasioned not by her daughter's behaviour but by her own.

Kathleen's initial reaction to the coming of the new ministry had been one of general pleasure combined with an assurance that it would not affect her personally in any way. This assumption was shattered one evening in Greenock when God Himself indicated clearly to her that she was to go forward for ministry. Though she resisted it at the time as an impossibility, she sensed during the next two weeks of inner struggle that she was being prepared for a real encounter with God. When she finally came for ministry, she felt that the depth of what God did in her was related to her obedience and willingness to go down on the floor whatever the cost to her feelings. She describes how He honoured her commitment by dealing with something from her past life:

> While I was on the floor the teenage years seemed to flash in front of me, and there was a tremendous sense of grief because I knew they had been spent far away from God and from His purposes for my life. Then a healing came in, and somehow those years were touched by God, and the hurt and the pain that had been involved in some of them was taken away.

Two weeks later Kathleen felt again a real need and an urge to respond to ministry. She was much more willing to do so this time. But she felt God saying, 'No, I want you to wait until tomorrow morning in Falkirk.' She had an awareness that God would move in the same kind of power in Falkirk as was operative in Greenock on Saturday nights.

> I felt so sure that God was going to do something that I almost phoned Jennifer in the morning to ask if she would come and pray with me during the service.
>
> Then I thought, 'No, I won't say that to her. If it's really of God then it will happen anyway.'
>
> And Jennifer did come to minister to me, which is quite unusual. As she prayed with me, I knew right away that I wanted to respond by getting up and out into the aisle. There came a glorious sense of mingled fire and light coming down upon me.
>
> The experience was beautiful and unforgettable.

Up to this point Kathleen felt it was by a somewhat gradual process that God had brought her into a deeper place. But there was nothing gradual about what happened next:

> Something quite new occurred in the Falkirk church a few Sunday nights ago. There was actually an outbreak of laughter, and I was very deeply involved in it. Part of me was quite horrified, because when I was brought up if you so much as coughed in the church you were scolded! There was a part of me very conscious that I was quite loud, but though I felt confused about it I couldn't stop it. The only way I can describe what I sensed in my spirit is to say it was like balls of laughter which were coming straight at me! They were bouncing along, and as they hit me I could feel all this laughter coming again. I was very conscious that there probably would be people there who would be struggling with it. In my own mind I was struggling with it myself, and I thought, 'If I could just be quiet...', but it was really loud! I was

disturbed myself by it, so I don't know how other people felt! But I could sense another ball coming, and then another.

'I really have to try and get a grip here,' I thought. 'This is quite unseemly in the church.'

Kathleen was genuinely perturbed at the thought that some might be upset or offended by her behaviour – and others perhaps tempted to imitate it. For these reasons she ultimately managed to restrain herself in the church. But God was not finished with her:

When we got home, Jack and I and Gillian sat talking over a cup of tea about what had been happening in the meeting. And all of a sudden another one hit me! We were all really hysterical! And we're not a family that just sit about and laugh! In fact, unless a humorous comment is very dry I don't find it remotely funny. Yet we were doubled up laughing. This time I was able to give myself to it, and found it tremendously uplifting: laughter that was sheer pleasure. I felt as though God had completed something to which I felt I couldn't give myself totally in the church, and it was really lovely.

Confusion arose in the week that followed. Still afraid that my laughing had disturbed and offended people, I desperately needed to understand why it had happened in church. I had read about John Wesley, who had a lot of problems with laughter, and I thought, 'If John Wesley had problems, maybe I shouldn't have let this happen!' Believing as I do that spiritual experiences are given for a reason – namely, for the purpose of change – I asked God if He would confirm to me in some way that what had happened was right – because I knew I couldn't stop it. I could actually sense those big, big balls just bouncing over!

The name 'Barnes Wallis' came into my mind.

'Where have I got this from?' I wondered.

The illustration is unusual, but it is the one that God gave me.

As I thought about it, I remembered that Barnes Wallis was the scientist who during the war designed the bouncing bomb. There were dams which were very inaccessible, and these dams had to be reached. God seemed to say that these laughter bombs had been designed to reach very inaccessible places.

And I now remembered that prior to Christmas God had said something else to me. I have suffered from clinical depression at different times, and this has always bothered me as something that should have no part in my life. There was one occasion when it had brought me into as black a hole as I can remember in my whole life. Just before Christmas God said to me, 'You will never suffer from this again.' That came back to my mind very strongly, and I felt as if God was saying, 'Yes, it was laughter bombs, and yes, they were to reach something that was very inaccessible, very deeply hidden in your spirit.' As they came in they seemed to be breaking up that hidden and inaccessible part, and I don't think this could have been achieved any other way – because the very opposite of depression is laughter and joy.

Commenting on the aftermath, Kathleen adds:

God did something very wonderful through that experience. Since that time I have come into a much freer, deeper place in worship. When we begin to sing in the Spirit, it is stepping into a river which is very alive and fast-flowing – it is Christ Himself. I feel as though the tunes of the songs that are coming are different, and I can remember them. A new tongue has been given in worship. It has all been related to that incident. There has been a freeing of something which was quite inaccessible.

But I'm just hoping that if these laughter balls come again it's not in the church! – because I think that people probably do have problems with it. Yet it did something very deep in my own life, and it reached an area of proneness to depression which had troubled me for a long time. God in a very wonderful and enjoyable way dealt with this.

The view of laughter as therapy is thus corroborated in this strikingly original testimony. More than two years later Kathleen asserts:

Since that experience of laughter, depression has never been an issue and I know it never will be – because the promise came first, then the experience and the change, and then the lasting effects. I know I will never succumb to this again.

Kathleen's concern about the appropriateness of laughter such as she describes in a public meeting is understandable. I myself had long known of the phenomenon of 'holy laughter', which is a glorious and healing thing. I have known people come into their baptism with laughter. But there is also a laughter of the flesh, and people can try to come into a spiritual experience by imitating something which is itself real. And so with weeping: there is a weeping that is real and deep and acceptable to God. There can also, however, be hysteria. It is for a wise leader to keep a gentle, quiet and loving eye on what is happening in a congregation, to curb that which is of the flesh, and to encourage that which is of the Spirit.

There can come, of course, a problem. If from the front a leader squashes a meeting because something has gone wrong, this can cause a flatness from which it will not easily recover. I have never personally attended a Toronto meeting, but I was present in one addressed by a speaker who had 'Toronto' connections. I remember being very relieved to hear him say of certain gatherings that when things took place that were out of order, the person or persons involved were quietly removed, not the whole company squashed. If the conduct was of God he reckoned that it normally continued, and if it was of the flesh it stopped, when they were out there in isolation.

In Kathleen's case the experience not only continued but actually deepened when she felt free in the privacy of her own home to give full vent to the renewed action of the Spirit within her. Her concern for others in the congregation was laudable; but one wonders what would have happened had an unwise leader quenched her laughter prematurely, or had her family circumstances not allowed her to give it free rein later. While the onlooker's attention may be riveted on the external phenomenon, the real action is taking place deep within, with consequences that are not transient but life-changing.

Testimonies to spiritual laughter offered a refreshing variety of comment on its benefits. For **Pete**, testifying a week after Gillian and Jennifer had spoken, it became both a means of access to God and a weapon in spiritual warfare. A few months earlier he had had a very significant experience under Diana's ministry in Cumbernauld.[4] He describes this before going on to speak about the coming of laughter:

> The first experience happened in a meeting a few months ago. We had had a Bible study, which I thoroughly enjoyed, but just before we turned to prayer I felt a real oppression and darkness come around me. I could not fight through it to find the presence of God – not even when Diana came to pray with me. So we went through to another room and continued praying there. There came then the freedom

that the sense of Christ's presence brings with it. And I give glory to God for that.

But as we were sitting there with the peace and the silence of Christ all around, and the sense of His light, I suddenly became aware of a very strong anointing coming on me that seemed to become physically heavier and heavier. It was almost like being covered by blankets that were slowly getting heavier until there came the point where I found my soul going right out into a place of worship that I had never been in before. The anointing grew so heavy that I couldn't stay in my seat, and I ended up falling on the floor. Now this was in a very 'grotty', dingy store cupboard adjoining the hall where we meet in Cumbernauld – but I just didn't care about that or about the fact that it was a cold night! I lay on the storeroom floor, conscious only of light all around, my soul going out and feeding, and worshipping in a place that I had never been in before. From that moment on there was a fairly significant effect on my spirit.

The other incident happened a few weeks ago; it made me able to relate so much to Gillian's experience of holy laughter. After a fairly tough week, it came to the Thursday night prayer meeting.

I thought, 'If I can just get through this prayer meeting, feeling the presence of God, then I'll be happy with that: just to sit in His presence, even with the assault that's going on around me' – in the words of D.L. Moody, to 'hold the fort'.

The prayer meeting hadn't been particularly rich up to that point. If anything it had been a bit of a struggle. When Diana came up and prayed with me I felt that I couldn't find a place of prayer or worship. As we continued praying, the barrier began to melt. I started to laugh, and couldn't stop laughing, until I was literally guffawing on my seat. A couple beside me had just started to laugh, and I think this had opened the floodgates within me. And even though it was in the prayer meeting I didn't care, because within the laughter there was the holiness of God; within the laughter there was a joy of God that I had never known before. It was starting to spill into the rest of the prayer meeting, and I think more or less everybody there that night ended up laughing!

But after the laughter had stopped the first time, I found there was a tremendous access into the presence of God, so much so that I felt my soul rising and rising, just wanting to worship Him and to drink in as much of God as I possibly could. It rose and rose and rose, and with that I found that my soul was longing to cast everything down before Him, cast all I was, every aspect of my life, before Him, until there was absolutely nothing of me that could prevent me from coming into His presence in the way that I felt opening at that very moment in time.

And just at that moment Diana prophesied. The theme of the prophecy was holy laughter, but the main aspect of the prophecy was that the enemy cannot stand holy laughter or endure its presence. And truly from the moment that I had started laughing, it was as though the enemy had fled, just like that. As Diana was giving utterance the laughter came back on me again, so that I think she actually struggled to carry on with the prophecy. There was a joy in the laughter that I had never known before, and I could relate so much of it to what Gillian was speaking about last week. Praise His Name.

✣ ✣ ✣

Another who had experienced laughter was **Linda**, a social worker. Her testimony, given a month after the event, speaks for itself:

When the new move of God came into the church I was very thrilled and pleased – for other people.

Though I found testimonies exceptionally helpful, I had apprehensions about going forward myself; to be honest, I found it a nightmare! But one night the thought came to me, 'This move of God is for the sake of the unsaved; it is for us to be blessed and then to overflow with the power of God.' And that became my desire. I was incredibly apprehensive. The only time in my life that I have ever gone forward voluntarily for ministry was when I was saved.

I didn't do too much talking about it at that point but went away and prayed, and the Lord spoke to me through the words of Jehoshaphat on the eve of battle:

> *'We do not know what to do, but our eyes are upon you.'* (2 Chronicles 20:12 NIV)

That became my desire: to have my eyes on Christ, to be really hungry for God. I found that as the weeks went past there grew a tremendous desire that was not natural, but God-given. I began to long for a real, dramatic move of God.

But then in the meetings something began to happen that perplexed me. Quite often when we sang in the Spirit, I suddenly discovered that I felt like laughing. And I thought, 'Good grief, you do not laugh in the church! You don't laugh as much as I feel I'm about to laugh! Contain it! Hold yourself steady!' Week after week I sat feeling, 'Oh, I'm going to laugh! Steady ... dodgy! Pull yourself back!' And when I did that, I found that the anointing would lift from my life and something was being lost.

Then one Monday night I found myself in the meeting in Greenock when Miss Mary Black was ministering. I had a tremendous hunger that put me in mind of how I felt when I was initially saved and baptized in the Spirit. Apparently Miss Black said, 'If people are looking for ministry...' and I don't know if I was in Mars, but I just never heard it. I opened my eyes to see a queue at the back of the room and thought, 'I need to be prayed with! I need to be there!' I was desperate for ministry! And everything happened to prevent it. There was no space on the carpet! I was thinking, 'I don't take up a lot of space, I'm really small! Surely there's got to be a small space left somewhere!' But there was none!

Eventually, however, a space was found, and when Mary prayed with me I came deeply under the anointing. I don't remember much about the ministry in itself; it's God I remember, it's Christ I remember coming. As we were praying I felt very, very gently a thin stream of light come down the left hand side of my body, and I knew (I'd felt it for a while) that I was about to laugh.

I thought, 'Oh, I'd better say something really spiritual and prepare somebody for this!' So I said, 'The joy of the Lord is my strength!'

And as that light came, it was as though it met years and years of adoration and worship that had been inhibited at that level. I laughed and I laughed and I laughed! I have never laughed so much in my life (even though I am quite a giggly person). It was tremendous.

I don't know at what time that happened, but I think I left the church at the back of ten – and I was still laughing at two in the morning. It was as real as that.

When that anointing had come and I was laughing on the floor, I felt as though Jesus had come to my right hand side and said, 'I will give thee back the years the locusts have eaten. And every grief and sorrow known shall be surpassed by My joy.'

Strangely – though Linda could not have known it then – the scripture she quoted was the one that had encouraged Gillian only the previous night in a different

part of the country. The second part of what Linda felt
Christ say was to come back to her a few weeks later in
circumstances that she did not dream of then. She simply
commented:

> It was tremendously real. I feel tonight the effects of
> what happened to me. Normally in attempting to
> speak in public I would be a nervous, gibbering
> wreck. Now I feel calm and anointed.
>
> What thrills me most is that I had an encounter
> with Christ, and I'm different, and it's tangible. Other
> people have sensed it. At work, two days after the
> experience, one social work student with a degree in
> psychology looked at me and remarked, 'I can't
> fathom it. You've got that born again look about
> you today, and it's awfully powerful!'
>
> And, you know, it's thrilling that I've got that born
> again look about me, because it is powerful, and it's
> real, and unsaved people have noticed. That is my
> desire: to see God move and not just bless us and
> revive us – but to see people converted. In my work
> I've found that people are interested. As recently as
> yesterday somebody said, 'I've heard there's a strange
> thing happening to people. People are laughing in
> meetings!' I said, 'Really?' I didn't tell them what
> happened to me, but I told them about Mike's
> miraculous healing: that has a tremendous attraction
> for everybody.[5] People are hungry for God. As a social
> worker I meet many, many people who are unsaved,
> and they are seeking for something. I am thrilled at
> what God is doing. It has taken me a long time to feel
> that I have come fully into the blessing. Even if I have
> to buy a new garment I take about a year to decide
> what colour I'd like! And in spiritual things I wait until
> the time is right. But I had my eyes fixed on Christ, and
> He deeply met me, for which I thank God.
>
> As I look to the future, I expect to see God move in
> the land of the living. Having seen it, I believe I'll see

more of it. And I really look to see people saved, set free and completely healed. Amen.

In Linda's case laughter had not only set her own spirit free to worship God, but had so changed her that her non-Christian colleagues were moved to comment. Like Gillian, she carried her experience on the church floor back into her work situation, and found that it made a difference.

It was to make a difference in an unrelated situation that arose three weeks later, when she learned that her uncle was seriously ill. A massive melanoma had been diagnosed behind his eye; it transpired shortly thereafter that he had terminal cancer. Linda sat at the bedside for the last 48 hours of his life, reading Scripture and singing to him. His last communication (she believes) was the smile he gave when she said, 'The angels are coming for you – do you know that?' She knew the moment Christ took him. Just as the touch of a 'thin stream of light' had set her own inner being free, so now there came a moment when she sensed a shaft of light touching the sufferer, and she knew he was gone – though technically still 'alive'. There came to her the words: 'Out of the night into glorious light Jesus has lifted me.'

It was during these last hours of her uncle's life that the memory came back to her of the words Christ had spoken as she lay on the floor: 'Every grief and sorrow known shall be surpassed by My joy.' So truly was this promise fulfilled in the mingling of natural grief with a greater joy that she hesitated to speak of it for fear of being mis-understood.

There was evidence that others also had been affected:

In his last two days my uncle shared a hospice room with two other men. The only privacy we had was a curtain drawn around his bed. Shortly before he medically passed away, one of the other patients beckoned to me and said, 'When my time comes I want to go like him.' It had not occurred to me that the two others had heard the psalms, the prayers and the singing, but (more importantly) I suspect they had felt Christ in the room. They would not have felt morbidity or indulgence because it was not there. Christ took control of that situation for us as a family, and this has been commented on by my mother and stepsister.'

Her concluding words were:

It was impossible for me to indulge in depths of grief that Christ had denied me. He afforded me joy and the privilege of sitting with someone I loved make their last journey in life. I can only conclude that God truly knows the end from the beginning.

Notes

[1] Gillian is alluding to Sarah's testimony, included in *A View from the Floor*, chapter 3. Sarah relates more of her experiences in this current volume, chapter 6.

[2] Jennifer Jack is minister of our Falkirk branch; her life story appears in my book *Consider Him (Twelve Qualities of Christ)* (New Dawn Books, 1988).

[3] Patrick Dixon, *Signs of Revival* (Kingsway Publications, 1994), pp. 70–2).

[4] Diana is featured in chapters 7 and 8 below.

[5] For Mike's healing, see *A View from the Floor*, chapter 4.

Chapter 3

Singing and Dancing

'Therefore they shall come and sing in the height of Zion, and shall flow together to the goodness of the Lord ... Then shall the virgin rejoice in the dance, both young men and old together.'

(Jeremiah 31:12–13)

The significance of a moving of God is not fully appreciated without some knowledge of the people amongst whom it occurs. We had always been a 'peculiar people': very vocal in worship but thoroughly Scottish in our distrust of exhibitionism, and in general very much on our guard against any kind of fleshly activity. Not for us the indiscriminate swaying and posturing that in some circles passed for spiritual 'dance'. Yet there were times when the company would be caught up in singing in tongues and the anointing would fall on some to worship in movement. They did so secure in the knowledge – or the hope! – that all eyes were closed! With the coming of the new ministry there grew an increasing freedom in the expression of our worship. This was not a by-product generated by the loosening of old restrictions; it was in itself a miraculous development that was influenced by the same breath of the Spirit as was felt in the ministry. While our attitude remained, as always, that the touch of the Spirit was essential, a number of people found that inner reserves were melting under His touch. The innerness of this phenomenon is revealed in the following reports, all given one Saturday night in Greenock in mid-March 1995.

The first, from **Jennifer Jack**, tells of developments in our Falkirk church. Since her original account of particular incidents concealed personal identities (including her own), I have supplied this and other information with her help and that of some of the others involved. Around the turn of the year Jennifer had felt that God wanted to do something new:

> On two occasions – once in the month of December, and then again on New Year's morning – the word came from Isaiah chapter 55, including the verse:
>
> > *'For my thoughts are not your thoughts, neither are your ways my ways, saith the LORD.'*
>
> The end of the chapter speaks about an abundance of life and growth and of the moving of God. These passages tied in closely with the word that was given to us at New Year, (*'If ye be willing and obedient, ye shall eat of the good of the land,'* and so on). There was the same thought of bounty. I felt that God was speaking about something new: that He wanted an openness in us towards Him.

Jennifer is referring here to the New Year Word, a scriptural promise that we felt God had given us at the beginning of 1995.[1]

Immediately after the New Year conference, in the first meeting that followed in Falkirk, Jennifer felt a difference:

> I was very conscious that Wednesday evening of something new that was moving amongst us. There were three different strands in it. One strand was song

in the Spirit, another was movement in the Spirit, and the third was the accuracy of the word of God. Now none of these things was new. We had had movement in the Spirit, song in the Spirit, and very accurate speaking of God in our midst. But I felt that a new dimension was opening up to us in all three of these ways, and they were all interconnected. I remember on that occasion there came a wave of song in the Spirit. Since then there has often come song with interpretation. As this has happened, there has been the sense of moving into a dimension where there is a greater release, a greater freedom and a greater abandoning of oneself to the Spirit.

There came a remarkable dovetailing of revelation. In the following incident, as Jennifer sang spontaneously in English, two of the company in different areas of the congregation received the knowledge of the words that were about to be sung and gave expression to them in movement:

As the song came, Kathleen had felt a desire to go silent before God, but to let herself be moved upon by the Holy Spirit. As the singing was taking place, the liberty for her came in expressing praise through movement. She had an accurate knowledge of the words that were going to be sung before they were sung, and that this was what was being expressed in worship through her own being as she moved. In a completely different part of the building Lesley, a co-worker, had actually gone down just before that under the anointing of God, and as the song began she knew the words that were spoken and began to move her arms in praise as she lay prostrate before God. In two different parts of the company there was an awareness of what God was going to speak about. And there was the sense of a different dimension that was indeed opening up.

45

Sometimes the revelation came in the closely timed ministering of identical scriptures, as in this case when Jennifer was leading from the front:

> At the end of that first meeting on the Wednesday evening there came that remarkable accuracy of the word of God. There was one person to whom God had spoken privately during the meeting about a situation in her life, reminding her of scriptures that she had already been given nine or ten months before. Ten minutes later, just at the end of the meeting, the same scriptures were quoted again, this time by me from the front, and they were quoted in the order in which they had been given by God – not the order in which they appear in the chapter. There was a tremendous sense of awe upon my spirit as these things were happening.

Time after time as the weeks continued there came the consciousness of a new dimension opening up during song and interpretation. Jennifer described how in one instance God gave someone a word about an incident that had occurred in the course of the day, and as the song and interpretation came there emerged confirmation of the word that had been given, without any kind of knowledge on the singer's part.

On another occasion God had spoken through two different individuals about His purpose to bring salvation to others. Gillian had sung of salvation coming from Zion's hill, and there followed a prophecy through another in confirmation. It was shortly after this that a significant number of people who were in contact with various of our Falkirk church members found Christ in a real and lasting way.

The other person in the story was **Ann**, who experienced a wonderful renewal of the joy of her own salvation. Happily married, with three toddlers, Ann loved her family dearly, but when she went down under ministry she wept very much in the presence of God as she felt Him speak about a loss of the initial joy that had accompanied her salvation – a loss that had occurred over the years through pressures of life. She sensed that this was an area to be put right. On a subsequent occasion in Glasgow when she went for ministry she felt that God said He would restore the joy of salvation. It did not happen at that time, but two days later in the Falkirk meeting, in the course of the worship at the end, there came that wave of song in the Spirit followed by interpretation. The words near the end of the song were of the joy of the Lord, and as the words were being sung, a wave of joy passed over her from the crown of her head down to the soles of her feet, and she began to laugh with the sheer joy and release of it.

The singer (who was Jennifer herself) knew nothing at all about what had gone beforehand, but after the meeting Ann said, 'God has changed something inside, and it happened as the song was coming forth in the Spirit.' For the sake of others she had tried to stifle her laughter, but to no avail – perhaps fortunately for the completion of the work that God was doing in her. Jennifer continues:

There has been an acute awareness of the dimension where you are free in song and in movement, whether it is going down before God or moving in praise and worship. In the worship time at the end of our Sunday service recently, when God was moving very richly, someone found that he reached a point where there was no liberty any longer in speaking or singing in tongues. But as he began to move his arms in worship to God, he found a tremendous anointing coming on him, and a knowledge that he was finding God as he was yielding to the moving of the Spirit in that particular way.

This is apparently a reference to Jack (chapter 4). Jennifer goes on to reflect on the general significance of the phenomenon of movement and song:

> The very first occasion that it happened was, I think, on the Wednesday after New Year. I found that as I was singing at the front as part of the company, it seemed impossible to stand still: it was almost as though one wanted even just to walk back and forth. It actually reminded me of an episode in one of C.S. Lewis's Narnian stories, *The Magician's Nephew*. The picture is of Aslan, who is the Christ figure in these tales. As creation was coming forth in that land, he sang and he moved back and forth, and as he moved and sang, things sprang into life. I felt there was something very similar. One was encountering a dimension where there was a tremendous creative life from God that was coming and touching us, and it was impossible to stay still, because there was so much sense of life in the atmosphere: a livingness, a growth, a movement. It reminds me of such parts of Scripture as:

> *'...the mountains and the hills shall break forth before you into singing, and all the trees of the field shall clap their hands.'*   (Isaiah 55:12)

There is a desire to move and to respond, because of the livingness of God in the midst.

During our Sunday night service Lesley described how she had had an inclination the previous week to have actions to a chorus that we never normally act out:

> He shall flow like a river, He shall fall as the rain,
>   He shall rise as the dawn in glory o'er the plain,
> And the knowledge of the Lord shall fill all the
>   earth
>   When the Spirit of the Lord shall flow.

'That's silly,' she had thought, and hadn't done it – but the actions had been clear in her mind. She explained the reason for it: in every part of her being she wanted to let there be a giving forth of praise, so that what was being sung could actually be expressed in movement. On this later occasion we responded to the chorus in that way, and there was an amazing sense of liberty.

At the end of the meeting I spoke a little about the whole idea of movement, and one or two people told me afterwards, 'I'm so glad you said that, because there's an enormous desire in me to be free to worship God, whether it is in song or in movement, whether He tells me to go down under the power of the Spirit, or to dance, or to laugh.' There is that feeling of wanting to know the freedom of the movement of God. There is wonderful liberty in that dimension.

It is only recently that I have begun to speak about it in Falkirk, because what I didn't want was people thinking, 'Oh, well, you know, you move, and you do such-and-such, and so you get into that dimension.' On the contrary, it is a touching of the dimension, and a responding to that which you are feeling coming on you, and it is a finding of God and then finding that expressing itself through you. We have found that numerous people are moving into this aspect of a new wave of the moving of the Spirit.

The importance of Jennifer's closing comments cannot be overrated. Flowing with the Spirit is an inner thing that has outward manifestation: it does not begin in the outer realm, nor does it consist of imitation of others.

In the next report, **Alison Speirs**[2] linked these new developments with what for us was a significant change in our church life: the move of the Saturday night meeting from Greenock to Glasgow. This was occasioned partly by the burgeoning size of the company that gathered at that particular service, but more importantly by a shared sense that the time had come to move to a more central location. The move was made after our Easter conference; but it was foreshadowed by a conference meeting in Glasgow one Saturday night in the middle of March. It is to this that Alison refers in her opening comments.

> Last Saturday night when we were in the Glasgow church (the conference moving there just for that evening), Mr Black's praying with me was totally unexpected. When he tapped me on the shoulder, I turned round and looked at him, supposing he wanted to have conversation with me. The next thing I was on the carpet, I think much to the shock of my catcher, who was winded on the road!
>
> But as I was down there, suddenly a sense of anointing and freedom came upon me, along with a knowledge that there was release in movement. I started to move my hands as I lay there. There was singing in the Spirit, and the consciousness of the anointing deepened upon me. I sensed that it was what God wanted for us as we moved our regular Saturday night meetings from Greenock into Glasgow. There was a knowledge that coming with that would be this freedom in dance, in worship, and in movement.

Meanwhile in Greenock itself the anointing for song and dance continued to fall. Alison describes two smaller meetings, in both of which a significant proportion of young adults and teenagers were present:

> Last Thursday night in our own house (where there is a prayer meeting to uphold the coming weekend), as we turned to God there was an amazing, beautiful and instant access into the deep presence of God that we all know and love so well. As it came, one felt the

freedom amongst the people. It was quite a small group, all of whom were very familiar friends. There was a feeling of safety and of being in a place where no one would be critical: I felt that was quite important. To the accompaniment of the guitar we started singing, 'Those who trust in the Lord are like mount Zion, which shall never be removed and which shall remain for ever.' At the same time quite a number of the people there started moving out in a new and a deeper, perhaps a more open way of dance than we have had. People have tended to remain on the same spot before, but there was a real movement not only of the hands and arms but of the feet and whole body as well. Three or four people moved out very deeply. The music continued into a singing in the Spirit. It was unutterably beautiful: that presence of God, deep and rich and full: what we all long for and know is there for us. I felt we sustained and stayed in it.

But I was even more delighted the following night when towards the end of our young people's meeting in Greenock as we turned to prayer again there was that same access to God, that same moving out in the Spirit, in dance and in the singing, and it was deeply, deeply beautiful. The song in the Spirit was accompanied by a phenomenon that reminded me of what Jennifer tells us of Falkirk (where two people knew the words that were going to come). In our case it was something I had never heard before: a song in the Spirit, in English, was beautifully accompanied by two of our guitarists. How could they know what was going to happen next, where the song was going to go? Simultaneously there was dance and movement to the song. I felt there was a wholeness to it, with the accompaniment, the singing, the dancing ... **and the sense of Christ that was there**.

Isn't that what it's all about? Somehow the deeper we move into that, the deeper grows that sense of the very presence of almighty God. As Jennifer says, it is a place of worship – and there is no doubt in my heart that it is deeply welcome before the throne of God, and that we who love Him can worship Him with a freedom that is not carnal, with a movement that is not of the flesh, but with our whole body, mind and spirit in subjection to that which is the desire of Christ.

Alison realized that what was possible in a relatively small gathering could happen also in a larger company:

Sensing the same spirit of worship again at the start of this meeting tonight, I rejoiced that it could come into a larger company, bringing unity to us, and that there is a trust. Where we gather together as a whole movement on a Saturday night, there is that feeling of freedom and a trust in one another that when we reveal the deepest love in our heart for Christ there will not be someone with one eye open thinking, 'Oh, look at her.' There is just an awareness that people are caught up in the Spirit. As it comes to us may we all be taken from the finite dimension into the dimension that is Christ.

She concluded with characteristic humour:

When I spoke of this to Mary (Black)[3] she laughed and said, 'Well, Alison, I suppose after we've all been lying down on the carpet beside one another, it does tend to break down barriers!' She's probably right. We can't be quite as formal as we once were, when we've all been falling between one another's boots, and so on! It breaks down those reserves that we maybe knew at one time. But isn't it lovely to know that as the body of Christ we are one in Him, and also, in that, one with one another? Blessed be His Name.

It is worth noting that the developments in Falkirk and Greenock as described by Jennifer and Alison happened independently of each other. One of the Falkirk congregation who thrilled to hear Alison's report was **Lesley**, whose testimony clearly demonstrates the spiritual significance of dancing in the Spirit as it came to her:

The first time that Jennifer moved out in song in the Spirit, I felt a tremendous liberty in my soul. Something so clear and wonderful opened up that I felt my whole being expand into it. I seemed to know the words, and for the first time there came into my head the thought, 'I want to act out what's being sung here.'

Having started to do it, I thought, 'This is really silly! Why should I act out what someone is singing?' Being particularly reserved in that direction, I just clammed up and said to myself, 'Lesley, stop thinking such strange thoughts. These things don't really happen' – although at the back of my mind was an idea that I had heard of it happening before. But the desire to do it had been so strong, so deep and so appealing, it was just as if my whole being wanted to be involved in it.

I spoke about it to Jennifer afterwards, and when she said that someone else had gone ahead and done it, I thought, 'Oh, that's typical of me, to end up thinking it just couldn't be right! Why should I stop what I feel is so real and so wonderful?' And so the next time the song in the Spirit came, I opened myself. No matter how strange one part of me found it, the other part just opened to allow the expression to come within.

It has been said that when people land on the carpet barriers are broken down. I have felt that in myself; as I have gone forward for ministry, and opened myself to God moving in that way, one thing that has happened in me is that barriers of self-consciousness have crumbled at a very deep level. This has been related to going out into that place where movement has become so clear and so full of the wonder of God: as the song in the Spirit comes, one actually moves into it and finds it very, very real. I have reached the stage where I want to go anywhere that the movement takes me. I'm not saying that I would be able to stand up with everyone watching me: that's going a bit too far! But (if everybody's eyes are shut!) I want to move with that expression and allow it to pour through my being, that God would take that place of pre-eminence.

Ultimately Lesley was able to put aside her embarrassment at the thought of public scrutiny when moving out in this way.

Commenting on how she had been prompted to ask the company to act out the chorus, 'He shall flow like a river', she explained:

While leading the singing of the chorus, I felt my being respond to it so deeply that I wanted to have the actions to it. I thought, 'Oh, I can't ask for actions to this chorus. It would sound ridiculous – I'd have to explain why, and I'm not really sure why.' But two weeks later, during the kids' choruses, it came on me again so strongly that I thought, 'So what?' I felt the expression so real that it would take us into a dimension where the whole of one's body, mind and spirit would be worshipping God. In doing the actions to the chorus my spirit moved out into a place of wonderful worship, giving everything to Christ. It was so beautiful: there has been such a release inside my whole being.

Commenting more recently on the anointing that she still finds for 'moving out' (in dance) to an utterance in English, where the movements coincide with or even anticipate the words spoken, Lesley made an observation that holds good for most, perhaps all, of us in whatever gift or ministry God has given: 'There is a tremendous anointing at the beginning. But to maintain that level of anointing I have to work at it: otherwise it will die the death.' She explained that this meant a constant openness and readiness to respond as the Holy Spirit might indicate, rather than sitting back with a careless attitude.

My daughter **Mary** commented on the point that had arisen about the breaking down of inhibitions. She said:

It is not really so much a question of breaking down inhibitions between us, although that is an overflow, obviously, of what happens when the inhibitions are broken down between our soul and God. I think what Alison and I were saying in conversation was that as you open yourself fully enough to God to allow Him to lay you down on a carpet (which for most of us, at least initially, is probably a difficult thing to do), then you can open many other parts of your being to Himself. And, yes, an overflow of that is that there is more fellowship and more interflow of the presence of God between the members, but the crucial thing is the breaking of the inhibition and self-consciousness between our soul and God. There are various ways in which God can do that. We can get used to many things, can't we? At first the idea of going down on the carpet was probably something that many people shrank from, but the danger is that it becomes the thing to do, and that God has to ask us to do something else that's completely unconventional and different from what we expect. We are so peculiarly made that we can adjust to whatever becomes the norm, and in our various ways we can still evade the point. We can still evade that vital touch of God which He is trying to communicate. We can come to the point of willingness to prostrate ourselves on the carpet, but we have still not broken this core of self-awareness and self-consciousness and wondering what other people will think.

I read once of a revival triggered by the obedience of a young girl who was told to go and strike a table. The presence of God was building up, and power was hanging in the air – and she was to go and bang the table three times. Now it must have seemed a very bizarre commandment to her, but in the action of obedience the power of God fell on the entire company. God is often more interested in the inner thing that is happening than in the outer event: that inner giving of obedience to Himself is vital and significant. For some people the breaking of that barrier comes in the moment of going down under the power, whether backward or forward. For some, kneeling is the action of humility that is required. And for some the release comes through movement in the Spirit.

Addressing the previous speaker, Mary added:

And, Lesley, I think God wants you to abandon your self-consciousness, and if He tells you, come right up here on the platform and do it any time! (They're all good people: they don't open their eyes anyway! – isn't that so?) The praise continues as we concentrate on God Himself.

Regrettably, it is not the case that an entire company can be trusted to be worshippers rather than spectators – and, quite apart from the possible self-consciousness of those who are moving out in worship, the quality of the atmosphere may suffer as a result. I am not saying that it is never right to open one's eyes during worship; what matters is the attitude of the worshipper. Those who come merely to watch and be entertained do nothing to help and are likely to hinder the progress of the meeting.

But for those with hearts to understand, the word is:

> *'The Lord has redeemed Jacob ... Therefore they shall come and sing in the height of Zion, and shall flow together to the goodness of the Lord ... Then shall the virgin rejoice in the dance, both young men and old together: for I will turn their mourning into joy...'* (Jeremiah 31:11–13)

As Mary said when speaking on these verses,

> Can you sense it? Can you sense the music in the air? Can you hear the melodies of heaven in the spiritual atmosphere? I believe what our speakers have said is true: there will be an increase of our catching of the very music of the high heavens. They will sing in the heights, and they shall flow together to the goodness of the Lord. Wherever the presence of God is, people are drawn as to a magnet.

Notes

[1] Over a period of years we had come to expect such a word. The verses for 1995 were Isaiah 1:12–19 and Psalm 132:13–16, supported by Psalm 133:1–3. There was in them a promise of abundance that was fulfilled in the experience of many that year. References to the New Year Word in this book are to the 1995 promise. See *A View from the Floor*, chapter 9, for the way in which the new ministry dovetailed with the word for 1994.

[2] Alison Speirs's life story appears in my book *Revival: Personal Encounters* (New Dawn Books, 1993), Part 2. Her personal testimony to the new ministry is in *A View from the Floor*, chapter 8.

[3] My daughter Mary's story appears in my book *Christian Fundamentals* (New Dawn Books, 1991), chapter 4.

Chapter 4

The Land of Christ

The action of the Spirit on the lives of those who received ministry was often directed to the meeting of practical needs, whether for healing (physical or spiritual), or for the equipping of their lives for service. The reader may by now have sensed that these outward benefits, wonderful though they were, did not lie at the centre of the new ministry, but were rather part of its outflow. At its heart was a particular revelation of God that was redolent with the atmosphere of heaven. The ministry was a door opening into that other dimension. Those who went through the door could be likened to travellers in a country hitherto unknown. With spiritual senses sharpened and spiritual perceptions heightened, some of them became aware of light, colour and movement that were not of earth, and always these spoke of Christ.

Of the hymns that came into being at this time, there was one above all that captured the attraction of that other realm. Entitled 'Within the Veil', part of it reads:

> There's a road that is open before us
> And it leads to a world unknown;
> Oft have we pondered its pleasures
> And pictured the heavenly throne.

We have thought of myriad angels,
Of harps and of jubilant song;
We have pictured our Lord and our Saviour
Where they praise Him all the day long.

But now our heavenly Guide
Is taking us upward from earth,
And we're entering spiritual hallways
With the sense of a spiritual birth.

There's a sensing of realms that we know not,
An acute awareness of need
To learn of the things of the Spirit,
To sit at God's table and feed.

The Lamb whom we pictured we see not
With the eyes of the flesh or our mind –
But we sense His ineffable nearness
As He opens the eyes of the blind.

Instruct us, our God and our Father,
As we move in this heavenly place;
Teach us the laws of the kingdom
As we bathe in Thy glory and grace.

Set our minds firmly on Jesus
As we search for that radiant face;
Let our feet go fervently forward
As we seek for that uttermost place.

Let it be clear that travellers in that upper dimension
were not to be written off as 'mystical types', head in the
clouds and feet nowhere touching the ground. The three
singled out in this chapter, all faithful servants of God,
were thoroughly immersed in the secular world. One is
Howard, a banker and father of three small children, very
active in church work, whether as a volunteer in the
church coffee shop or as a street evangelist with a Teen
Challenge bus. On Saturday 19 November 1994 Howard
did not know that a new ministry was to dawn that very

evening in our church services north of the border, but he had already made up his mind to seek ministry that night, as he explained a few days later:

On Saturday morning I felt the unction of the Holy Spirit to go for prayer that evening. Without knowing what form the meeting would take, I knew that I would be going out for ministry, to get into the place of walking under the anointing of God, where the Holy Spirit creates miracle in people's lives.

Drawing me in that direction were two incidents in our own home the previous weekend. My daughter Jennifer and my wife Sheila had both been unwell. At such times we ask the Lord in faith to touch and to heal. On this particular Sunday night, Jennifer was healed instantly of a cold. Sheila was brought closer to Christ, and I felt there was an element of deliverance there. In our home, healing of that nature isn't unusual; but this element of deliverance, of the purity of light coming in, thrilled me. It was beyond my realm of experience with Christ and the Holy Spirit. I thought, 'This is something extra.'

The following Friday saw some of us at a meeting in Darvel, where Mr Black was speaking about drawing the church into a place of action in Christ. As he spoke the words, 'Do, do, **do** for Christ,' my spirit leapt within me. I was affected too by a vision I saw on the same night of a river that ran into a sea of light. I seemed to go through the light, and beyond the light I saw a Man: it was Christ Himself. His white raiment spread out endlessly and became a sea, an ocean. I didn't understand that fully until the Saturday night – which was the first time in Scotland Mr Black called on people to go out for what was to become known as the 'new ministry'.

Because there was such a leading up to it, I really wanted to respond – but like so many others I quaked. For a few moments as I stood on the

platform there was a feeling of alienation, as if I
didn't belong there, until I saw two acquaintances and
felt peace in going to stand by them. Shutting my
eyes, I raised my hand to the Lord. As I prayed in the
Spirit, my knees started to go. I wanted to sit or lie
down, but was conscious of the platform steps behind
me and did not want to fall back. As it happened,
while Mr Black was praying for somebody to the right
of me, he unintentionally touched me in the stomach
with his elbow. At that, a phenomenal burst of light
came in! Then he took me out into the aisle and
prayed, just lightly touching me. The only word I was
really conscious of hearing was 'anointing'. As that
happened I went right out. All I saw was (as it
seemed) a ring of something going over my spirit,
and the next thing I knew was that I was falling back
on to the floor. I felt I had a choice either to get up
and go back to my seat, or to stay where I was. I
decided to stay. The carpet on which I lay became
the softest, warmest, most beautiful I've ever known.
The love of God that came through, the ocean of the
fathomless love of God, was unforgettable. As I speak
of it, I can feel it gently coming back: oceans and
oceans, depth beyond depth of God's love to all His
people.

I sat for a long time in the church, wanting to drink
in as much of that love as I possibly could. I would
have stayed there all night if I had had the choice.
Sheila drove us home, because I still had wobbly
knees and couldn't trust myself with the car. In fact I
didn't want to do ordinary things; I just wanted to
remain in the love of God as long as I possibly could.
As I got out of the car my eye fell on the sticker on
the back bumper, with the words 'Jesus is Lord'. I
saw His Name, and as I spoke it, it was again as if a
ring, or wave, of electricity, came up over me. For
those few moments, though it was dark and raining
and probably cold, I was in the most gloriously warm,

sunny blue day. It was more real than the natural world. On becoming more aware of everyday things, I said to Sheila, 'Why are the lights off? Why is it dark?'

I want to live in the reality of the land of Christ; I don't want to live here any more. I want to know the life of the land of Christ. And I want to die to myself enough to live in that reality, where my life doesn't really matter because I know I have life eternal in His land. That's where I want to be.

'I want to die to myself enough to live in that reality': there is here no question of evading the responsibilities of this life in order to prolong a pleasant experience in another realm. In like vein Howard continues:

But during the week following that Saturday night's experience I started to feel a need for greater holiness. I wasn't particularly sinful, but something in my flesh was wrong. This brought me into a place where I had to give up another bit of myself. As I did that, the warmth that seemed to be receding came back. Now I want to live in that reality, surrounded by that blue, sunny day all the time. Praise His Name.

The link between heaven and holiness is clear even in this overwhelming encounter with the world of Christ. And – to drive the point home – the last time I saw Howard he was on his knees scrubbing someone's kitchen floor!

Pearl, like Howard, is no stranger to scrubbing floors or any other of the domestic tasks involved in raising a large family, besides caring for others in her profession as a nurse. Also like Howard, she takes an active interest in evangelism. Though she does not specify any particular trouble, she had known an unusual amount of life's pain – a relevant part of the background to her account:

Last Saturday night when Mr Black prayed with me I remember just lying on the floor and there were tears and tears and tears – I was conscious that I didn't have a handkerchief! The tears were flowing, and as I lay there Christ drew very, very near in a way that I had never known Him before. The tears also were different: they were tears of joy, and with them I could sense there came a healing.

As Christ drew near, I could sense such wonderful colours, beautiful colours, and the brightest of all was a shimmering gold. It was a colour that I could hardly describe, it was so beautiful. I couldn't keep my eyes from it. There were other colours round about it, but this one was peculiarly significant.

Christ's coming was like a baptism of love: wave upon wave of His love just surrounded me. I was conscious of Christ as never before, and there were lots of things that I could have said to Him, but He was so precious at that moment that everything else faded into insignificance. His love and seeing Him was just enough. I was very conscious of that chorus, 'His face shall outshine them all,' and for me it was absolutely wonderful. This week has been so precious and so different. Praise His Name!

It was 'as Christ drew near' that the beauty and colour of that land were revealed, for He Himself is the glory of Immanuel's land. A very similar revelation had come in the early months of 1995 to one of our Falkirk congregation, **Jack**, whose secular occupation is with an oil company. The revelation came in stages. His first encounter with the new ministry is described initially in down-to-earth terms:

For some time before the New Year conference there were areas of my life marked by anxiety or ill-ease: areas of misgiving. I think everybody experiences that from time to time; why they come into your life may not be so important as the fact that they are there and difficult to cope with. All the time that these things were in the background and sometimes very much in the foreground, there was at the same time a consciousness of the reality of Christ in my life. There were specific things that I would pray for and ask the Lord to handle or give me grace to have strength to work through, and Christ would work in a very miraculous way. I would look at these things and say, 'That could only be done by the touch of Christ Himself; the Holy Spirit must have touched that, and changed that situation, or given me the grace to be able to work through it.' There was that sense of the reality of Christ in my life. And so both these aspects would appear to be in tension. I'm sure you understand what I am trying to say; it is a common enough experience.

At the conference meeting in Greenock on the Saturday night, as always the praise and worship particularly attracted me. Yet at the same time there was that sense in the background of misgivings and apprehension. It was a felt thing, as I tried to reach out for God. There didn't seem to be the freedom that I sometimes experienced in praise.

The next development was unexpected. It began as Jack attended his Sunday morning service in Falkirk:

About three-quarters of the way through the meeting I began to feel pain in my hip, and by the end it was really sore. There seemed no rhyme nor reason: it apparently just happened. By evening the pain was excruciating; I could hardly move. I lay all that night on the floor. I couldn't come downstairs in my own house, far less down to the meeting in Greenock.

But around eleven o'clock, before my wife and daughter came back from the meeting, the phone rang. It was Mr Black, who had heard about my predicament, and he said, 'We'll just pray about that.'

Now there wasn't a physical healing, but what really came over to me as I put down the phone was the compassion of Christ. I was lying there on the floor all alone, feeling very sorry for myself; and into that situation Christ spoke of His understanding about where I was, the pain I was feeling, and His compassion for me. That was all expressed through Mr Black – and it was a tremendous thing. It was as if the Holy Spirit Himself came in and touched me. Though there was no physical healing, inside it was as if somebody had given me a lift.

The next night I was able to come to the conference. Tucked away in the corner, I felt perfectly safe, until towards the end of the meeting Mr Black sent a metaphorical nudge along the row where I was sitting: 'Come on out!'

'Oh, my goodness!' I thought – because I have never been one to go forward easily for ministry. There has always been that reluctance in my spirit. I think very early on in my spiritual life somebody had said to me, 'If you seek God with all your heart, then you'll find Him.' And as I consider going forward for ministry there is always that doubt: 'If I am seeking God with all my heart, do I really need to go forward here?' So it was not without apprehension that I came out from my safe corner.

Mr Black took my arms, and as I was going to turn and face him he said, 'No, turn that other way.' Another member of the ministry team was standing there. And in the way that inane thoughts flash through one's mind, I thought, 'Oh, this is going to be great – if I do collapse here, Mr Black's going to catch me – seventy-odd years old, and he's going to be catching me! So what happens if I kill him? I'll need to leave the church!'

But in a moment it passed. As we began to pray, there was a going out in the Spirit, a leaving of the place where I was, and a diminishing awareness of the people around me and of what was happening. I was aware of the more immediate group of people who were praying for me, and of Christ Himself. Facing down against the slant of the aisle, I was conscious at one point of being determinedly poised on my heels and thinking that I could assert myself mentally and put myself back on my feet. Now Mr Black said at that point, 'Go all the way with Him.' They had been speaking about healing as they prayed for me. At the time I didn't know whether Mr Black was speaking to me, or whether it was part of his request for Christ to go all the way with me. But it triggered something in me, and I thought, 'Yes, that's right. Go all the way with Christ.'

And it seemed as if I passed from all consciousness of where I was in the physical realm into a vast place, a place of great peace and tranquillity, where I felt that Christ ministered to me. How long that lasted in real terms I don't know, but it seemed a long time. Then I became more aware of my physical surroundings again. As I spoke to Mr Black afterwards, there was a great easing of the physical symptoms of my hip. I wouldn't have said at that time that I had been healed; nor would I say even now that there was a miraculous healing of the pain in my hip. But nonetheless I believe that Christ cut through all that: He knew what I really needed ministry for, and He went to the very heart of my situation and brought me into a place of great space and great peace.

One senses here the entry into a new dimension. The next stage in Jack's testimony followed fairly quickly. Beginning with an allusion to his wife Kathleen's testimony (chapter 2) he says:

It would indeed seem to be a time when God is touching parts in people that are inaccessible, the parts that we can keep a tight rein on: our inhibitions.

One inhibition I have always had was about movement in worship. In a charismatic church we used to attend, most of the worship would be earmarked by movement in the front three rows while I in pedestrian fashion would be nearer the back of the church. I was happy that these people found worship and praise in that way; but it wasn't for me.

But there comes a stage in your life when you recognize that there must be a deeper way to reach God, a deeper way to express your love and appreciation for what He has done in your life: you want to reach out with everything you've got. I very much wanted to do that in a way that would be pleasing to God, and I wasn't sure how to go about it or how to express this desire.

An inkling came one evening in Greenock during a time of praise and ministry when the piano was being played in the Spirit. At such times the music itself seems to be set free: without written music, there is a spontaneous outburst of praise in the Spirit. It was a beautiful time. And as the music played, in spiritual vision I could see different colours. They were far stronger than we would normally see in everyday life: strong, individual colours, and yet they would come together and then go apart – though independent they also seemed to be interdependent upon one another. As I looked at them, the colours danced as if they themselves were in worship. It was an absolutely beautiful thing to see. It was not that the colours outlined different objects: they were beings in themselves, if you can understand what I'm trying to say. It is a very difficult thing to try to convey. In the Bible when people saw visions they would often say, 'Well, it was like this,' or, 'It appeared like that.' I often feel that language falls far short of conveying spiritual experience. But it was a felt thing, a real thing, something that you could reach out and see in your spirit, and it was a beautiful and an amazing thing.

I thought, 'Lord, that's just the realm I want to be in. I want to be set free as these colours are free – to move and to praise and adore you in a way that is absolutely free.'

Nothing happened for a short interval until we were back at Greenock again. I had been expressing to the Lord my desire to move in that way. What happened then reminded me of a game you may have played when you were younger, where you link your fingers with someone else's so as to take the weight off your arms and achieve a kind of weightless movement. During the time of praise it was as if someone came and put their fingers on top of my fingers, took my hands and began to move my arms. It was a tremendously freeing thing. I found that I was in praise and worship to the Lord, just moving my arms and the upper part of my body. It was not a physical but a spiritual setting free. Although it was a limited thing bodily, in my spirit it was all movement – and a complete freedom in movement. It was the kind of thing where you say, 'Oh, Lord, I don't want to go back to where I was before; I want to stay in that realm. I just want to praise and worship You, and enter into more of that realm.'

I could hardly wait till Sunday morning. Very quickly I was in that place again as we came to the time of praise. But this time as we began to praise and worship I could see a procession coming through all these colours. I was reminded of the Song of Songs, and the thought that came to me was, 'Here comes a procession with the King of kings surrounded by an angelic host.' I could see that in my spirit, and I could see the colours. Again I had that very definite feeling of someone or something with their fingers on top of mine. And as I began to move my arms in praise and worship and looked at my hands again, there were colours surrounding them and seeming to dance all around me. Remembering how the Bible says all creation is held in captivity, the thought came strongly to me that there is a level of spiritual freedom where all creation is set free, and a realm of worship where there is a complete freedom, and you are at one worshipping with creation, you are an interdependent part of everything, and everything is glorifying God in praise and worship.

These are unusual testimonies. Lest some readers have been wondering, 'What's all this about **colours**? I thought that was New Age!' it is important to notice the Christ-centred motivation and focus throughout the testimonies. The potency of New Age philosophy is that it tunes into themes that **are** universal in their truth and significance. But whereas it typically claims, for example, that 'all is one' and does not take evil seriously, Christianity maintains that only Christ can redeem and unify a fallen creation through the atonement. The realm into which the givers of these testimonies were taken was not just another aspect of this present realm (corrupt and doomed to destruction), nor was it a psychedelic 'trip' induced by drugs or occult means. It represented a glimpse into something that cannot be adequately pictured by the human mind but that is laid up for us in Christ.

As for the particular images mentioned – light, colour, oneness, interdependence, and so forth – to be sure, every one is found in New Age philosophies. They are also prominent in both Old and New Testaments, in images such as the rainbow and amber and sapphire of Ezekiel's visions (stranger by far than any represented in our book), the Light of the world (John 8:12), the whole creation in travail (Romans 8:22), members of the body of Christ (e.g. Ephesians 5:30) and of each other (*ibid.* 4:25). Having said all this, I would warn the reader: do not seek after such experiences for their own sake. Read again the testimonies, and note how one and all glorify God through

Christ. There is a legitimate hunger for the realm where Christ is revealed and glorified – a realm of miracle and often unusual phenomena – but only when He is central.

> The bride eyes not her garments,
>   But her dear bridegroom's face;
> I will not gaze at glory
>   But on my king of grace.

The loving heart knows how to reject the false and accept the true. For Samuel Rutherford, who inspired these lines of A.R. Cousin's, it could almost be said that no metaphors were too extravagant to describe his perception of Christ and His kingdom – but this was because it was true for him that

> The Lamb is all the glory
> Of Immanuel's land.

Chapter 5

But I Can't Possibly Do That!

'And what sort of church do you go to, Bill?'

That was the type of question I was usually asked by a fellow accountant I might have met on a business trip down south – often a Baptist, perhaps even someone baptized in the Spirit. I would hasten to reassure him.

'Oh, I go to a pentecostal church – but it's not one of those pentecostal churches where they dance in the aisles and fall down! We're not like that!'

Bill was able to laugh at himself – eventually – when his stock response was suddenly removed from his armoury. But not at first.

One of the most telling features of the new move of the Spirit was its diversity. While some were finding release in song, laughter and dance, others found God probing in ways that were distinctly uncomfortable. For Bill, the changes he saw in church life were initially a shock. The new ministry, which he could not help but recognize as valid, and to which he had even responded himself on one or two occasions, inaugurated a period of inner struggle:

As I opened myself to God, I saw the reality of it. The testimonies of other people were particularly helpful.

In spite of that, I was really struggling for a few months. In our house we developed a strange set-up, in a classic case of the tail wagging the dog. Traditionally in the Scottish churches if the young people go at all it tends to be the result of parents persuading or dragging them along. In my case, without my realizing it, the enthusiasm and commitment of my own children was the main reason that I went along – because I found it quite hard to attend some of the meetings, but felt responsible to encourage the family.

Deep down I think I knew the reason for the struggle. It was nothing to do with the new movement, because I knew that was of God. The problem (to be blunt) was my attitude towards some of my fellow Christians. This saddened me greatly. I prayed to God that He would take this away, and I suppose what I really wanted was that some day God would, spiritually speaking, wave a magic wand, and the problem would be gone! But it didn't happen.

Even one of my favourite activities was affected. I have always liked open-air meetings. It is a great privilege to be in the open air testifying for God and praising Him. So what if more people are laughing at us than are laughing at others? It has never really bothered me or dampened my enthusiasm. But recently I found it a great struggle to go, for example, to the Glasgow outreaches. The underlying reason was my wrong attitude; but I had buried the knowledge away, and didn't really think much about it, hoping I would waken up one day and it would be gone.

There came a particularly difficult weekend at the beginning of April 1995, when Bill had attended the monthly Saturday afternoon outreach in Glasgow mainly for the family's sake. On Sunday night, he thought, he would stay in and rest.

What made me change my mind (to my shame) was that if I hadn't gone I knew that my son Douglas would have rushed into the house after the meeting, and his first words would have been, 'Dad, why weren't you at the meeting?' That didn't seem the best way to encourage our young people. So I went along and struggled through the first part of the meeting.

Then Bill's attention was arrested by a testimony that had a strangely familiar ring. It came from another parent:

He described how on the previous Sunday night he had quietly walked out of the church with his jacket and gone for a walk, coming back at the end to pick up his youngsters. He had gone for ministry and been prayed with, but God had shown him there was a ceiling there, and until certain things were changed he wouldn't get through this ceiling. Somehow, I couldn't really have said why, this aroused a great interest in me.

Much to his own surprise, when the invitation for ministry was given Bill put up his hand.

I had been out once or twice before, and tended to have a preconception as to how God might move. Mr Black had said that recently God had been very kind and gentle with us as a people, and I had heard others testifying about seeing great lights and wonderful colours and so on. My attitude was that I had been struggling along, doing my best, and if anything happened God would sort of pat me on the head and tell me what a good boy I had been and I was doing my bit and trying, etc., etc.

When I went down on the floor, I felt God speak very clearly to me. What He said, and what He asked me to do, shocked me.

'I can't do that. It's not fair, God, asking me to do something like that!'

He had shown me very clearly how wrong was my attitude towards certain things in the character of another Christian – really, I hadn't particularly liked these aspects for years. Not only that (and that was fair enough), but He asked me, when I got up off that floor, to go and speak to the person, to tell him exactly how I had been feeling for years, and to tell him that God wanted us to pray together, and that the barrier was just not to be.

God may have been dealing with many of us very gently, but that was not my experience. What I felt was something I had never felt before, and it was so very real: it was the irritation of God – really, the abhorrence that God has of any disunity among His people. I had never felt it so real. There was an irritation: there was no gentleness or anything like it. I felt this very clearly for myself – but I suspected that perhaps it was for us as a church as well.

When God asked me to do this, my first reaction was, 'I can't.' God showed me that ceiling that had been spoken about, and made it very clear that there was no way I would go through any spiritual ceiling until I had sorted this out within my character. I couldn't do it. There are certain things in life you find easy, and certain things you find hard. Even in the domestic sphere, if a workman hasn't done a job right, I hate embarrassing, one-to-one confrontations. My wife Margaret does a much better job than I – so she usually does it, and I go and hide in the garage or somewhere!

I really don't think I could have done it, but for one thing. It came to me that we are all links in God's chain, and the fact that my relationship with this person wasn't right was hindering God's work. That's an awful thing: if you think about it, that's a terrible thing. It really bothered me – and it convinced me that I had to do this. But the thought appalled me.

I got up, and the first thing I did was look for Mr Black – but he wasn't any help at all. When I told him, 'God's asked me to do something. He's asked me to go and speak to somebody,' I suppose I was hoping he would say, 'Well, we'll maybe pray about it,' or 'We'll maybe think about it, Bill.'

But he just said, 'Oh, it's nice to do it at the time.' Then he wandered off and left me! No doubt for good reasons, but...!

I watched Bill with great interest, for all that!

In trepidation I went and said to the person concerned, 'Excuse me, could we talk somewhere privately? And could we pray about something?'

And, you know, this thing that had seemed a terrible barrier and an awful thing to have to do, was not hard! I am not saying we should do it willy-nilly: we should only do it when God tells us very clearly. But it was not nearly as hard as I had thought it would be. We sat down, and I explained how I had felt, how God had shown me how wrong it was, and that He wanted that barrier broken asunder. In a strange way the other person seemed almost pleased. His attitude was very gracious, and I praise God for it. We turned to prayer together.

Now I'm not one of these people that feels physical sorts of things. Probably I could have counted on one hand the number of times I had felt anything like a physical sensation accompanying spiritual experience in my previous eighteen years as a Christian. But as we prayed together, the power of God came down in a phenomenal way. I was absolutely shaking. Not only was that barrier between us burst asunder, but I knew in my spirit that a bond was built between us, and it was a spiritual thing; it was something that only God could do.

The experience showed me very clearly that any

small things that separate us are quite irrelevant compared to the things that unite us, above all our common desire to tell people about God and glorify and praise Him. That became so clear to me. And when my friend and I got up after praying we did a very un-Struthers thing, but I felt it was justified on the occasion: we gave each other a big hug!

It is a terrible thing that we should in any way hinder God's work. That was certainly one chain which was broken asunder. If there had been adverse feelings towards any other, they simply disappeared. In a personal sense, a great burden was lifted off my shoulders. I felt free in a way that I had probably never felt before, and I thank God for doing all that He did.

The passage of two and a half years has proved the reality of God's work in Bill that night. The attitudes which he had striven in vain to alter were decisively transformed by the grace of God and by Bill's subsequent obedience to the instruction given.

One of the scriptures that had been brought to our attention at the beginning of 1995 was Psalm 133, beginning,

> *'Behold, how good and how pleasant it is for brethren to dwell together in unity.'*

We had also been promised that if we were 'willing and obedient', we should 'eat the good of the land'. On the very same Sunday that Bill finally awoke to the discovery of these truths, God was speaking to **Janice** along somewhat similar lines. Janice does not specify what the problem was, beyond the fact that it involved others besides herself. Like Bill, she had been aware of something being out of kilter over a period:

God had been speaking to me for about a year, but I had shied away from it constantly. As for the new ministry – it frightened the life out of me! Though unable to deny that God was moving very deeply in it, such was my own spiritual dearth that as time went on I was beginning to look round the church and think, 'Maybe this is not for me.' (That I should have thought such a thing really disgusts me now!)

Before going to church one Sunday morning I asked God to speak to me through a specific person, either personally or through a word in the meeting. The person concerned did in fact come over to me at the end. I took the word given, knowing God was speaking to me. And then in the course of an interpretation God spoke about how we were to face what He was showing us, and that He would deal with it in love and not in condemnation. I knew what He was saying.

On the Tuesday morning, thinking of how she had not felt His presence in her life for about ten months, Janice prayed, 'God, set me free that I might worship You in spirit and in truth.'

Later that morning she drove a few miles down the coast to Lunderston Bay, intending to have a coffee in the garden centre there. But as she sat in the car park, the dismal, grey weather outside reflecting her mood, she felt she could not wait any longer to have things put right. Turning the car, she drove back to the church bookshop in Greenock and was very soon in my office seeking help.

I told Mr Black how I hadn't been feeling the presence of God.

He said, 'What is the cause of that, Janice?'

I explained what God had been saying to me.

Mr Black took me into the church hall, where we prayed. God broke right through my reservations about the new ministry. I had no other option, and

He knew the situation that was in my life had to get sorted. It was sin; having heard God speaking to me about it for so long, I couldn't take it any more. If I wanted to go on with Him, this thing had to go.

Before I knew it I was 'on the deck'. God moved very deeply in my life. I got up a completely different person. While I was on the floor, God showed me that I had to go and speak to certain individuals. When I got up I was terrified, thinking, 'I can't do it! I'm such a weakling – I can't do it!' But God said He would give me the strength to do it. And praise Him, He did! I was able to approach the people concerned with the problem that God put His finger on.

The result of her obedience to the voice of God was what Janice called a 'total clearing out' of the blockage from her own life and a renewal of the sense of God within her.

✥   ✥   ✥

For many, the act of obedience required was nothing further than going forward for ministry at the Spirit's prompting. Again and again we heard testimonies re-iterating how personal fear or doubt in this respect were overcome and totally swept away in the joy that came with obedience. In this sense **Pauline R** was a typical example. What was not typical was that she was one of the last people whom one would have expected to be governed by fear of any kind.

For most of her young life as the only girl in a family of boys, she had learned toughness at an early age. One is tempted to tell some of the anecdotes that help to define Pauline's character, but we'll just mention an early visit of Pauline's to our Glasgow church, Knightswood, which was motivated by a desire to have a bit of fun. She had heard that the congregation was led by a female minister, a teacher to boot. Pauline's main experience of teachers had been to see how far she could 'take the mickey' before getting 'flung out' of the classroom. As she and her friends sat with intent in the middle of the front row under the pulpit so that the 'teacher' would see them, she reflected that no member of that unfortunate profession had ever been able to control her. The question at the back of her mind was, 'Is God any different?'

Gathering her forces for the attack, she raised her eyes to encounter those of the said minister, and received the shock of her life.

'It was Christ's eyes I saw looking out at me!'

Mary (for it was she) had simply looked briefly over the congregation as she announced the opening hymn. She had not particularly stared at the young hoodlum sitting immediately below; yet the moment when their eyes met seemed to Pauline to last for five minutes, during which she saw not Mary but Christ. She sat frozen, and still had not moved at the end of the service when most of the company had dispersed. Interrogated by her astonished friends, she could only say, 'That woman has got something!' She very soon found Christ for herself, and her life changed dramatically – though not her reputation for fearlessness.

But now as she sat listening to yet another testimony to the new ministry, all she could think was, 'Oh, Kate, will you be quiet and sit down!' As she explains:

> It was not the first time I had had to listen to someone describing what sounded uncomfortably like my own experience.
>
> In the beginning I had been wide open to the new ministry, seeing that God was really meeting people in the church. That was fine – so long as I wasn't asked to go out. When I did feel I was to go, my reaction was, 'No way!' And for a long time this continued to be my response.
>
> To begin with I wasn't sure what it was that was holding me back. Then one day it hit me that the reason was fear. It's not often you'll hear me saying

that I'm scared – but I was! I was really afraid of going out because I knew that I was coming in contact, not with Mr Black or any other human minister, but with God Himself. I knew what I was like and simply felt, 'I can't go out there!'

And now another Sunday night had come – and it seemed that Kate would never stop speaking.

Just as the praying started Mr Black, who I think had previous information about how I was feeling, came up to me and enquired, 'Where's your bottle?' [1]

I replied, 'You can say anything to me – I'm still not getting up!'

At the end of the prayer time he practically dragged me out. (It wasn't that I didn't want to go ... I was just scared.)

As I went down I felt a total acceptance in God – just the love that God has for me as an individual.

Up until the point when I went for prayer, I had been closed to the moving of the Spirit of God. It wasn't something that I tried to do: it happened because of the disobedience over getting up for ministry. But since I went out it's as if my spirit is wide, wide open again, and I am free.

Those who feared the Divine Surgeon's knife found the gentleness of His dealing. Even if He probed uncomfortably deep, His healing balm flowed swiftly in. Two testimonies in the next chapter indicate the tenderness of His dealing with those who carried pain deep within their being and were set gloriously free by the Master's touch.

Note

[1] This is an expression calculated to put a person on his or her mettle! – HB

Chapter 6

Rise Up, My Love

'I may not be renowned for my shouting,' said **Effie** (she wasn't), 'but driving home from work on Tuesday I was so glad I was in the car, for I was **shouting** – literally shouting for joy!'

A conspicuously upright member of the Christian community and leader of our Edinburgh fellowship, Effie had just had one of the most profound experiences of her life. One of the most moving aspects of the new ministry was its ability to touch deep inner need. With a minimum of human counselling, Christ Himself came to bring relief from burdens carried for years. Small wonder that Effie was glad of the privacy of her car:

> With folk around me at work and at home all the time, I have been jumping into my car this week just to get away where I can be free to shout aloud for joy.

Inevitably Effie was reminded of the promise that had been given to the church at the beginning of 1995 (chapter 3):

> Through all the good things God has been doing, particularly over the past few weeks, the New Year Word has been speaking very deeply into my heart, particularly the promise that Zion's *priests shall be*

clothed with salvation. That has caught my spirit and is really blessing me. I was very drawn also to the words, *And her saints shall shout aloud for joy* – and now that is being fulfilled!

God has been working very deeply over the past months, particularly since last August. Over that period of time I have been amazed at the perfection of God's workings and His ways with an individual life. The amazement is not because one didn't know that about God, but because of the loveliness of the experience and seeing how perfectly God works things and brings the details together.

What He looked for from me was obedience. Obedience has been a very large key to my moving on in what God has been wanting to do. And so some of the things I have been doing over the past few months have been very businesslike – I've just had to gird my loins and do things very contrary to the 'me' that I am. But I have known each time I have taken a step of obedience to God it has been part of His work in opening me up to Himself and making a way for Him in my life, and I really thank God for that.

As the song has it, 'If the Lord had not been on our side, would we still be here today?' That is a very real question. I feel so deeply in my spirit the sense of God and the call of God over the years, His graciousness and His goodness. The holding of God on a life is wonderful.

In a way that may remind the reader of Jack's testimony in chapter 4, Effie describes the strange duality of her experience over the preceding weeks:

Since New Year there has been a stream of blessing flowing for us in Edinburgh. I have been conscious of its deepening and thankful for it. But at the same time I have been like two people – rejoicing and seeking to go forward in what God was doing, and yet becoming increasingly aware of an area of my life that I had kept bumping into over many years. It was very deep down inside, and I had puzzled around it on many occasions. I knew that somehow, in a way that I couldn't fully understand, it was the area that God wanted to get right into and deal with at this present time in His way. And I honestly didn't know what to do about it. You know how you feel you've done everything you can do, you've prayed all you can pray, and there it is: just sort of **there**. It wasn't a problem to God, but it was a big problem to me. This is where the preliminary steps of obedience were so important in letting Him come further and further in.

I had some consciousness of the areas around which this was centred, and about ten days ago I was becoming increasingly desperate, but with a desperation that had in it a real, certain knowledge that God was working and would not leave me in that condition. His purpose was to change me and to have His way. As I waited before Him, a number of words came to me. Two of them were **unfinished** and **incomplete**. That was exactly how I felt. Now I know there is a sense in which until the day we go to heaven we'll be unfinished and incomplete, but this revelation was particular to what God was wanting to do. And the other two words were, **grief** and **sorrow**. These words really quickened in me. I knew that they described the area where God was wanting to move. There had been over many years a number of situations where grief and sorrow had entered my life. Sometimes indeed I had given way to inordinate grief and allowed it to lodge very deeply in my spirit. (I had on more than one occasion listened intently when Mary or Mr Black had spoken on the subject of excessive grief.) I am sure it was at the prompting of the Holy Spirit that I decided to take action. The lovely thing is that God led me this way because He knew me – He deals so faithfully, kindly and gently with lives.

And so I wrote a letter to Mr Black.

Now I am an abysmal correspondent, as anybody who has been waiting to hear from me will know, and yet I had three pages filled in no time. I was able under the Holy Spirit to write it down. This was not only helpful to me; it was very important that I should commit myself to what God was wanting to do.

Amongst other things the letter described how for more years than I could remember, no matter what else was happening, I always had an area around me like a grey fog. It would never move, though it wasn't even a hard obstacle. I would go so far and would just seem to get into this fog and not be able to do anything about it.

In Greenock the following weekend I encouraged Effie to come forward for ministry at the appropriate time. She describes how she did so, first on the Saturday night, then again two nights later:

Getting up out of my seat, I could hardly stand for the weight of God's presence and the anointing. Under ministry I went down and was before God for quite a time, in some ways not knowing what was happening, but just abiding there. Though not understanding, I was aware that God had worked the next step.

In the course of the Monday morning at work an immense urgency came upon my spirit. I was content to let God do His work in His own way and in His own time. But suddenly the knowledge came that it was God's time and there wasn't to be any more time wasted by me. And so I phoned Mr Black up at lunchtime and more or less said, 'Help!'

'Come through to the Monday night meeting,' he said.

There was a lovely presence of God as I came in. As we went into the time of prayer, my spirit was drawn out to Him in love and worship. Mary came and ministered to me, and there was the wonderful attraction of Christ, expressed in words from the Song of Solomon:

> *'My beloved spoke unto me and said, Rise up, my fair one, come away.'* [1]

I could feel my whole spirit responding, 'Yes, that's it, Lord. That's what I want – that's what my heart's longing for; that's what it's all about.' And I let my spirit go out to God.

Then Mr Black said, 'Come, and we'll pray for you.'

So we went up on to the platform. And the minute we started to pray I felt my whole being break up inside, and I was down on the carpet; then, wave after wave, I was breaking my heart and crying from the very depths of my being. It was very painful, as though something was being wrenched out of me. But at the same time I knew God was working, and there was a sense of real, deep control. Then it became quiet, the meeting ended, and I went to sit in one of the seats.

At that point Grace Gault, who had come to pray with me when I was on the floor, began to speak to me. Some of this is very, very personal, but I think it is important that I say it, because it is part of what I was and what God was wanting to change. Grace had been conscious that there were things being unknotted and released. But she said, 'It's not finished.' She was conscious that somewhere along the line when I was down on the carpet I had pulled back. Now I wasn't particularly aware of doing that, but there was probably a fundamental inability to go any further at that point. And she spoke of a deep inner reserve which was containing all this need to let God in there. There was an aspect of my personality, my character, my being, that was reserved – which I knew to be true – but it was also reserved towards God. It wasn't allowing Him to get in there and touch that part and do the very thing that was needed. It is completely contradictory, when you think about it! But the human heart, the human personality, does this sort of thing. There is a great big bit of self there, of course: it is self that is reserved. So one has no illusions: it is not something to be proud of. As Grace was speaking I knew she was revealing truth, and afresh with all my being I wanted God, wanted Him to be in me as He wanted to be.

We prayed again, and in that moment there was the completion of the work that God had been working in me over many months, probably over many years. It was very real. The beauty and the loveliness of Christ was there, and I have been drawn out to love and adore Him.

I stayed overnight with Grace, which was a real balm of healing. (I don't think I could have driven back, anyway.) In the morning we prayed again, and the words came, *You shall not pass this way again.* I had passed that way so often! But I knew in my spirit that was the word of the Lord, and I wouldn't pass that way again. The night before I had been reading the Song of Solomon – and of course after the invitation, *Rise up, my loved one, come away*, comes the assurance, *The rain is over, the winter is past, the time of the singing of the birds has come.* And yes, it has, and it is utterly lovely. I have been so conscious of that this week, and cannot do justice to what God has done. I just know that He has come into me in a way that I knew was needed but didn't know how to find. He has broken up the depths within, and that area of reserve has gone. There is a communion and a fellowship and a love of God, a knowing of Christ, a confidence born, and a newness, a freshness.

I went to our own Thursday night meeting with a tremendous sense of expectation, and God came amongst us in a wonderful way such as I had never known before. A lady who had been saved weeks earlier was baptized in the Holy Spirit, and you could see that she was literally being transformed, the light of God shining into her heart. One of the deepest longings of my spirit had been for what God wanted to do for others in Edinburgh. We have gone on for a number of long years, but I feel that the heavens have opened now, and that He is moving, and I just thank Him with all my heart.

It must, I imagine, be evident to most readers by now that God has been doing a very deep work in hearts: not superficial, not just touching the surface, but going down deep into the personality, changing things that we could never change. I think He will continue to do that. This is what revival means. It is 'coming to life'. In a case like Effie's, most people would have said about some of the things that were troubling her, 'Well, it's just part of your nature.' There are many things that are part of our nature that God does not want to remain: He wants to change them. God changes people, He changes circumstances, He changes us to the very depth of our being, and He makes us complete in Christ. As you open your spirit to the action of God, prepare to be changed into the image of Christ Himself, into the likeness of Jesus, changed to that depth.

✠ ✠ ✠

The kind of inner healing that took place in Effie's life did not always happen so quickly. For some it was a process marked by progressive stages of ministry. So it was for **Sarah**, who was not quite out of her teens when the Spirit began to move amongst us in this way.

Sarah's first experience of the new ministry is told in *A View from the Floor*. There she describes how her initial terror at what she saw happening around her gave way to the overwhelming reassurance of Christ's presence with her as she lay on the carpet. In that moment, she says, all fear of the ministry was taken away and a door opened for God to begin moving in her life at a new depth.

A few weeks later she found herself unexpectedly receiving the same kind of ministry again, this time from Alison Speirs in the Greenock youth meeting.

> Had I known that Alison was going to ask us to step into the aisle, I would not have put my hand up so readily!
>
> When she prayed with me, a strange thing happened. I went down on the floor, but all I was aware of was pain and grief inside, though I wasn't immediately sure what it was or what was causing the pain. I let God do His work, and by the time I got up at the end of the meeting I knew that He was dealing with a hurt that I had carried for about ten years. It was a burden of guilt concerning a situation for which I had blamed myself from about nine years of age, due to something that had been said to me. It was in itself a very painful circumstance, but it was a lot harder because of the feeling of guilt. Though the situation could not possibly have been my fault, I blamed myself every time it arose.
>
> I knew that God hadn't finished dealing with it; He had just touched it and made it sore. Over the next few meetings I went forward for prayer so that God would continue the work He was doing.

Meanwhile there was a very different matter that God wanted to deal with. He drew it to Sarah's attention through a testimony that has since been published in *A View from the Floor*. She explains:

Two weeks ago, when Elaine was giving testimony to a friendship that was restored to her, I knew that God was bringing up yet another matter in my life. It was a relationship that had been badly marred. We had attempted several times ourselves to sort it out, going before God and trying again – but it had just never worked. Now I knew that God was giving us an opportunity. I told the one concerned what I felt God was saying to me. We prayed together and let it all settle, waiting to see how God would lead us from there.

These two situations – grief with a sense of guilt from the past, and a difficult relationship in the present – formed part of the background to what happened for Sarah one unforgettable night in February 1995. The occasion was made memorable, among other reasons, by the fact that she received prayer no less than five times!

When Miss (Mary) Black gave an invitation for ministry, I had a slight struggle in my mind, thinking, 'I've already been prayed with three times, and what more can God do in one meeting?' However, I knew that I should respond. And just as I was walking up to the back I felt a tremendous sense of anointing coming all over me; but it was different from the other times I had been for prayer. Miss Black came over to minister to me, and I struggled for a minute, because I could feel the weight of the anointing of God, but at the same time I knew in my heart that God didn't want me to go down on the floor at that point although I was finding it quite hard to stay up. Just then she said to me, 'Sarah, take your freedom however it comes.' And I began to move out in dance. I had done this before but not to the level that God opened to me that night. What happened next was absolutely incredible. For a long time I had struggled to believe that God loved me and that His

91

call was on my life. And just in moving out in the dance I found that level after level of my being was beginning at long last to open up to God. That went on for quite a while; I was just dancing, utterly amazed at what God was doing, and at how deeply He had come inside me.

Then there wasn't enough space on the floor, and so I had to be shifted. Slightly jolted, I felt as though for a few moments I had lost the thread of what was happening. This, remember, is the meeting I was prayed for five times – and four times down the road here I was standing, not sure what to do next!

Along came Alison and began to pray with me. In one part of my mind I thought, 'I must be in a really bad way if I need five people to pray with me!'

But she said, 'Just go right out to God – He is going to work a real miracle for you tonight.' I sensed what the miracle was, and that it was to open my being up to His love and to open parts of me that never before had I been able to open because of pain and circumstances which He was now healing.

Just like that I was down on the floor, and it was different again from anything I had ever experienced before. The presence of God came exceedingly close to me. Even in the going down I felt that a door had swung wide open in my heart, and the love of God came flooding in as I had never known. The weight of God's presence that came on me was unbelievable and indescribable. It was as though it just pressed me on to the floor, and I could neither move nor get up nor do anything. I began to pour out praise and worship to God. And in the pouring out of praise His healing came right inside me.

'I didn't know this was possible,' I thought.

I had not realized that one could know the love of God like that and have such a depth of being open to Him. At first I wasn't quite sure what to do because I was so utterly overcome with God: it was just God.

Doing the best I could, I began to move out in tongues.

And then, in a way that I cannot explain, something inside me changed. Even my speaking in tongues changed. I knew in that moment that I was free. All the hurts and the difficulties of years were gone – situation after situation had been exposed and healed. I was pouring out love and worship to Christ in a way that I never had been able to do before. The love of God had come into my heart at a level that I had not known was possible. My heart was open to God at long last in the way I had yearned for. Whereas I had not been able to touch the part that was scarred and closed over, He just put His hand in and opened it up and poured in of His love and healing. Unable to move, I lay on the floor soaking in that unutterably beautiful love. In my mind was the thought, 'When I get up from this floor I am going to be different.' I knew that everything inside was changed and all the pain taken away.

I got up eventually and felt completely different. Though I was not altogether sure what God had done, I knew that there had been a healing and a restoration. As the days went on I found an unprecedented freedom and access to God. I don't know how many people actually live in that; I had not known it was possible.

The relationship that had been so difficult was totally healed. More than that, there came a unity, a joining with one another in spiritual places, that God had meant us to have all along.

Sarah also found a new attitude to the cross in her life:

Whereas before it had always been difficult to die to self, and I could never find a place of victory or peace over the situations that God was asking me to face, after having been down on the floor being operated

on by God, although there was still the pain of dying
to self, at the same time there came a great sweetness.
In the next few days the situations that had caused
such pain and difficulty, and even had the power to
take away my communion with God and surround
me in utter darkness, did so no longer. Instead there
was light all around the cross, and light all around the
situations. Yes, they were painful; yes, God was
asking me to die to them at a deeper level; but there
was just such a light – that is the only way I can
describe it – and such a beauty and a sweetness. While
I still felt the pain of having to face these things, at the
same time there was an incredible sense of the love of
God and of deep security, and a knowledge that
Christ had come right into that deep part of my being
as I had longed He would do. He Himself had
removed all the hindrances and had given me a place
of absolute freedom, a place of the knowledge of the
love of God and the call of God on my life. I don't
say that in a proud way. He is leading me by a path of
humility, showing me what it is to walk under the
anointing, and it is not a matter of pride to do so
when you know the anointing is there. It is not proud
to move out and do what God is asking you to do. I
feel as though a whole big chunk of self has been
taken away and the anointing of God is flowing, and
the love of God is flowing, and I'm free.

One of the differences this experience made to Sarah's
life was in her ability to let the Holy Spirit minister to her:

The healing of these things in my life opened something in my heart that had never been opened to God
before. There came a night when I received ministry
again and felt wave upon wave of the love of God.
Instead of coming only so far and then meeting a
blockage, it came right inside with no pain or hurt to
stop it. I went down again into the sense of that love

and into the depth of Christ's presence. But on rising I felt as though it was not complete: there was something yet to happen.

Two nights later again I received ministry. Not quite sure at first what was happening, I did not understand why I was crying. Then the presence of Christ drew very close to me, and I knelt down.

As I was on my knees, I saw Christ coming towards me. It wasn't a vague feeling of the presence of Christ coming towards me; it was with my spiritual eyes I saw Him coming right in front of me. He put His hand out to me, and I felt that in spirit I just took a hold of that hand, and we began to walk through places I didn't know – like the courtrooms of heaven. We began, Christ and I together, I holding on to Him, to walk through these places. And I began to be filled with an incredible sense of joy and peace and a knowledge that at long last my heart had found Christ. The person who was ministering to me came back to me, and just said these words to me: 'Christ has found you, and He'll never let you go.' And I knew that there was such a pleasure in the heart of Christ. For so long, I suppose, He had longed to come into me at that depth and I hadn't been able to let Him. It was not deliberate; it was something that I couldn't help and He had to deal with. In those moments I knew that He had taken everything away, and He Himself had come right inside. There was a union, a bond that wasn't there before. I knew that I had found Christ and that Christ had found me, and that there was a bond of love between us that never need be severed again. Never again need I go from pillar to post looking for that love, or looking for Christ, because He had so come and had so joined Himself to me that I felt we never could be parted.

Around this time Sarah began to enter more deeply into her call. An anointing increased for ministry of various kinds, in worship, in outreach and in youth work. Like others of her generation at this time, Sarah was being prepared for a life of service that should have communion with Christ at its heart. Without the healing ministry of Christ to her soul as she was 'on the floor', there would have been no such road forward.

Note

[1] The biblical quotations on pp. 87 and 88 are paraphrased from the Authorised Version.

Chapter 7

Patterns Old and New

The new ministry had been operating in our midst for about two months when **Susan** pinned me down one day in the church coffee shop and addressed a question to me. A down-to-earth Scotswoman whom despite my maturer years I affectionately call my 'granny', she is a very direct lady. Her question was not on the new ministry as such, for she acknowledged that God was in it, but on an issue of moment to one of her tradition.

'Why', she asked, 'did you not preach from the Word last Saturday night? I came to hear the Word – not your words!'

It had in fact come sharply to my attention that there were times that God did not wish me to preach when I was normally expected to do so, and I would have been wrong to persist in trying to preach. At certain moments I knew clearly, 'The power and the glory of God are here, and God wants to move without preaching.' On the occasion in question there had indeed been no sermon in the sense of exposition of a given passage of Scripture. Instead I had spent about twenty minutes commenting on the worldwide moving of God and preparing the congregation for their own experience on what I often described as His 'operating table'. My remarks had been followed by testimonies contributing to the same end.

I explained to Susan that Scots people particularly may

hold a very wrong idea about preaching. It lies in our history from the time of the reformation. In the Scots Presbyterian (perhaps rather more than in the Anglican) tradition, the sermon was regarded as indispensable. If I myself had not valued sermons I would not have been preaching them for the past fifty years! But it is easy to get a wrong view of their function. We think of the sermon as an object in itself, to be criticized, accepted, admired, rejected – in short as something that exists in its own right and for its own sake. And that is not true. The point of a sermon is to produce action, normally to produce change. If a company is instructed again and again along the same lines, there comes a point where there is no more need to go on speaking but there is need to enter into the thing that God is opening. The preaching is over, and one prepares for action.

For my friend Susan, the hour had come to take the next step. There had been quite enough preaching for her along one particular line. And she accepted that. She understood and thanked me for the explanation.

At the weekend Susan was drawn to come for ministry, but because of possible transport difficulty she went away early. She arrived home just in time for a shocking incident next door, which caused her to have a very troubled week. However, she came for ministry a week later.

> I must admit, when Mr Black first started practising this way of ministry in the church on a Saturday night that God had so graciously given him, I doubted it. I wondered about it; I pondered it. And finally I got before God and came to the conclusion: 'Yes. This is of God. But it is not for me.'
>
> And then three doors away from where I live a man was shot. It was a drug-related shooting. After putting in quite a traumatic week, I thought I would go for ministry – but didn't. So last Saturday night I decided, 'Yes, I will.' Then I thought, 'No, I won't!' When Mr Black asked people who wanted ministry to

put their hands up, I folded my arms and refused to move. Then as he came up the aisle I thought, 'Oh, yes, Lord, I will,' because I felt the urge on my spirit that I was to go. And I am glad now that I obeyed the urge of the Spirit to get up and stand there.

I remember Mr Black coming up the aisle; I don't think he touched me at all. I heard the one word: **Jesus**. And that was the last I heard before going back. I don't even remember going down. But as I lay there – as I must have lain there because I definitely wasn't in this realm or this world – I felt all the stress and strain and the pain of years being, as it were, gently massaged away. Have you ever had a pain such as a headache and you massaged it? That's what it was like. It was like a gentle massaging of my soul and my spirit. And as the pain and the hurt was being smoothed away, in came the healing and the peace of God.

It was so wonderful that I actually thought I was in heaven. I realized that I hadn't a care. The Lord had set me free from all of it; the hurts and ills of years had gone. He had set me completely free. I lay there laughing with the joy of it, the joy that had come to my soul because the Lord had released me from all the stress and strain, and all the worries and cares of this world. It was so lovely I could have lain there all night. Hearing singing, I thought, 'Oh, this is wonderful – I am in heaven!' I thought it was the angels singing! Then my eyes opened and I sat up. And the first face I saw was Mr Black's, and I knew I wasn't in heaven!

In all seriousness, I did not sleep all Saturday night with the wonder of what the Lord had done for me. Just think about it for a moment: me, nobody. And there He was: the mighty God, the King of Kings, the Lord of Lords, my Lord, and He came down to heal me, to minister to me. Isn't it wonderful? I think so. It is glorious what the Lord has done for me, and I am glad now to speak about it – even if I did change my seat and hide in the middle of people so that Mr Black would not find me – but he sought me and he found me! To God I give all the praise, honour and glory for what He has done.

Let it be emphasized that when God speaks to us it is not with a view to our putting what He says on a record and merely playing it ever and anon: 'That's what God said to me.' What did we do with what God said to us? Why do we expect God to speak to us again and again if we have not obeyed what He has already said? It is vital to get preaching into its right perspective.

Around the same time as my friend Susan was accusing me of shortchanging the people, another of our leaders, **Diana**, was occasionally giving her Cumbernauld congregation even less change in conventional coinage. She too recognized that there was a time to preach, and a time not to preach but to let the glory of God fall directly on men and women. So great was that glory that at times she herself could not stand to minister.

She describes the coming of the cloud of glory over the people:

> I want to go back about four weeks to the beginning of the new line of ministry that has come on a Saturday night. The first night that it came to Greenock, in spite of the distracting element of being seated right at the front I found that my spirit was very deeply affected. I went home not quite sure what I felt, except that inside there was a glory that I had never sensed before, and a particular access to God that I had known only at very special times when God was very, very close to us. It seemed to me as though heaven itself had come closer. On the Sunday morning and Sunday night in Cumbernauld I noticed that the same glory had come to our meeting. There

was the same sense of that presence of God, and it was wonderful. I kept myself open at a mind level in case God would move in that same way and in fact indicated to the people that perhaps He would one day, but that I didn't work the way Mr Black worked, nor could I, and we would just need to wait and see if the Spirit would come that way. And I left it at that.

The following Sunday again there was the same atmosphere, the same deep, deep presence of God, the same sense of the glory with us. I began to be aware of a cloud of glory coming over not just over our own movement, but over a wider scene, and it was as though we were catching the edges of that. Again there was an opening in my spirit and a marked access to God, with revelation and discernment over different issues in certain lives. On a Sunday night we have a tarry time, and the ministry that night was very powerful, with quite clear indications from God.

I had to go south for five days, and became aware of having moved out of the cloud. It wasn't that I had done something wrong, but there was a geographical factor, and the glory wasn't there. On my way back up last Saturday, I wondered when again I would feel the cloud: would it be next Saturday night?

In fact it was in our first Sunday morning service, within hours of our return to Cumbernauld, that I became aware of that glory again, and we had a wonderful meeting. I did not have liberty to preach; all the 'preaching' came through in prophecy and revelation, which was much nicer for me – and the company probably preferred it as well!

That evening the effects of the cloud of glory began to be more fully manifest:

I was aware again of that glory, and preached and turned to prayer. Leading from the front, I became

aware that the atmosphere was becoming charged
with the power of God (the feeling was almost of
electricity), and there was no more need to lead the
company: they were already going through. The Holy
Spirit indicated to me to go to one lady, saying before
I went that she would receive deliverance – and it was
indeed a lovely deliverance. Just at the point of being
set free she went prostrate under the power of God. I
watched her for a minute or two before moving away,
and her face was absolutely radiant. She is quite a
reserved young person, of a slightly withdrawn nature
– not the very outgoing type that I so often meet
nowadays. But she was totally oblivious to everything
that was going on in that meeting, and you could
see that she was in communion with Christ. Her face
was alight with the glory of God. She had come from
a fairly bad situation where she had been in quite a lot
of trouble, and God changed her life that night.

I then felt the Spirit very clearly indicate to go to
another, and again it was as though the heavens were
opened to that one; the power of anointing that I felt
on myself was absolutely wonderful, and again that
person went down. And then the Spirit indicated
another two, who both went down as well. One thing
I liked about it was that it didn't distract anybody; I
don't think people in the Cumbernauld company were
aware that it had happened, unless they opened their
eyes and looked. There was a lovely sense of it just
being part of the meeting, as natural as eating bread
and butter. There was no feeling of, 'Oh, what's
happening here?' There was just a feeling of it being
so right to be in the presence of our heavenly Father
that way.

I later asked the first lady to testify to what had
happened. She said something lovely: she had felt
Christ was standing in front of her, and she was in
communion with Him; there was just no block
between her soul and Christ, and she didn't want to

come out of that place. At the end of the meeting (in a public hall) we had had to clear away the keyboard and chairs. People were carrying furniture over her head, and she wasn't aware of any of it going on as far as I knew. At the end I had asked somebody to go and help her up, because we had to be out by a certain time. She had begun to weep – tears both of joy at what had happened to her, and also of regret at having to come out of that deep inner place of worship. I felt it was very, very real. The change in her life has been lovely, and I do hope it will continue.

Finally, Diana describes the first of Pete's experiences (chapter 2) from her point of view:

In a mid-week meeting I was ministering to a man who had come under fearful assault, as happened from time to time, and not in relation to things that he had done. I believed that he would come into ministry in time and that God was preparing his life for that. We went through to another room to pray together, and again the revelation was very strong. I saw a demon and heard it speak to me; I then saw Christ come in between the man's life and the entity, and I saw the soul being drawn into the love of Christ. In the moment the love of Christ came, the evil thing could remain in the room no longer and had to go. The power of the assault was broken, and the presence of God was almost tangible in the room. When we had finished praying we sat quietly together in the atmosphere, not talking, both with eyes still shut, and still basking in that deep presence of God.

Suddenly I began to feel again the coming of that presence, that sense of glory, that anointing that I had felt on the Sunday night. I could feel the weight of it on myself as it began to come over me. I said nothing at all to my companion, but very quietly began to whisper in tongues. As we both worshipped, he went down under the power of God and went out much further than he had been before. He went out into a dimension of God, a dimension of reality, and it felt to me almost as though flesh itself had passed away and we were in the eternal presence of the living God. It was wonderful. Something for me that night was clinched – the feeling of the anointing, the familiarity of that sense of the coming of God in that way – and, without any words spoken, the person who was receiving ministry recognizing the anointing and going with it. Afterwards he did say that he had felt coming on him the weight of the glory of God, and there was such an ache of desire within him for God that he could no longer remain on his seat and went down under that weight. I felt as though God filled every part of his being with Himself.

Chapter 8

When the Priests Could not Stand to Minister

In January the manifestation of God's presence in the new ministry continued in Cumbernauld. In one instance a girl was spontaneously healed of an ear condition. Diana described the event two weeks later:

> The girl had been suffering for a month from pain and loss of hearing in her ear. Prescribing a second course of antibiotics, the doctor had said that if the condition did not clear up the next stage would be a referral to the Ear, Nose and Throat Hospital. Half-way through her second course she came for ministry. When she went down she felt a hand touch her ear, she felt something happen inside, and she was able to hear again. She was visibly moved by it when telling me. I felt that it was very real. She has not been a Christian long and I think it encouraged her to realize that Christ had actually touched her physically. This meant a great deal to her.

The following weekend Diana's sister-in-law **Gail** experienced a phenomenal visitation. As Diana tells it, there was an amusing side to this story. Again there had been no sermon:

Last Sunday night I never got round to preaching. The Spirit fell during the singing, and it just was not suitable to preach. I had given an invitation for ministry and felt quite a strong draw to pray with Gail. Hesitating to do so at the beginning of the ministry, I prayed with all the others who had responded. At the end I opened my spirit again, to find the urge still very strongly there. When I went up to her, she was already getting so far through into the presence of God that I was a little reluctant to interrupt and call her out into the aisle. Gail is a very self-effacing person, and I wasn't quite sure how she would react to being 'brought out' of her time of worship in such an abrupt way. But in fact the draw was so strong that I went with it.

She came with me and we began to pray. Almost immediately the power of the Spirit began to fall on her. I wasn't touching her, but just praying, standing beside her, going through into the presence of God. I could see light coming all round her; her whole being was like a sponge absorbing that light. Then there came something like a bolt of light from heaven and it struck her. She went down like a pack of cards. It was lovely: just at that point I opened my eyes to see her going down, and she was laughing.

Then the power hit me and I suddenly realized that I also was going down and could do nothing to stop it! As I tried to turn round and catch on to a chair behind to steady myself, I went right down and started to laugh because of the sheer joy and exhilaration at God's not only meeting Gail, but touching me in the process as well! I was wearing a radio mike, and all I could hear was the sound of my own laughter coming through the speaker beside me! Putting my hand over the mike, I tried to hold on to a chair. Though I had to go down I instinctively knew that I was catching the overflow of blessing on another, and it was for me to get up and go on ministering.

Speaking to Gail afterwards, I did not tell her what I had seen or felt, but just asked her, 'What did you feel?'

Using the very imagery that had come to me, she said, 'I felt like a sponge, and I felt as though I was just absorbing light.'

She noted that she had begun to stagger almost as soon as she was up on her feet. The strange thing was that she had been on her feet before leaving the seated area, but when she came out into the aisle it seemed that more power began to hit her, causing her to stagger. Though aware that she could hardly stand, she was determined to stay there and get as much of God as she possibly could, until, she said, 'I saw as though a bolt of lightning came out of heaven, and it struck my body, and I went down with it.'

Speaking later to the one catching her, I asked him, 'Did you feel anything of it?' thinking that if I had felt the power of it he must have done so also. And indeed he also saw the same bolt of light come down and touch her, and felt the same power coming on his own life.

I have felt more and more to encourage certain people not to go down too soon, but to wait for the deep power of the Spirit to come. Although there can be times when you feel the gentle draw of the Spirit and you go down willingly with that, I love it when the Holy Spirit comes and puts a person down at the point where they couldn't stay on their feet even if they tried.

Although Diana was constrained to continue ministering in this instance, there came a later occasion when she herself went down under the power of God. It was not the first time she had been 'slain in the Holy Spirit' while taking a meeting:

> The first occasion was about two and a half or three years ago in a prayer meeting – one of our smaller meetings in Cumbernauld. At the time I was under fearful assault. As the presence of God came in, I felt as though my physical being couldn't stand the conflict, and without any thought of going down I found myself on the floor unable to move for over an hour. I let God do His work, I let the conflict break, and rose up in victory. Though I never fully understood what it was all about, there came with it an awesome presence of God. One person there thought I had actually died, and was frightened to open her eyes in case there really was a dead body lying at her feet!

Diana felt that this experience, which she had not shared with anyone at the time, had rendered her more open than many others to the new ministry. On the other hand, so aware was she of God's presence with her that she did not feel drawn to come for ministry on her own account. In this her experience was very similar to Pauline Anderson's as told in *A View from the Floor*.[1] But there was something for Diana too, and it came in a most unusual way – again during a service she herself was taking. She recounted the event a few days later:

> On the Monday I normally like a day off, not from spiritual things, but from people's problems, just to be quiet and alone with God. For some reason, two weeks ago I never got that. Every day seemed to be full of people phoning, people arriving at the door, people with problems. By the end of the week I felt very drained. And in fact it was almost my desire last Saturday night to stay at home just to prepare and be refilled for the Sunday. But there were people coming

for ministry, and I had to be present at the Glasgow service.

A young woman approached me at the end and said, 'I want you to pray with me, and I want you to pray that I'll go down under the power of the Spirit, but I don't want to **go** down – I want **the Holy Spirit** to **force** me to go down.'

In her reluctance to fall before she was compelled there is another reminder of Pauline, although in this instance the background was very different, as Diana explains:

Now this lady had been out for ministry before in Greenock. The Holy Spirit had told her to go forward, and when she did so she had felt the anointing come on her to go down. Yielding to that anointing, she had a wonderful experience. God had brought her into a place of worship that I had always longed that she should find. She had been truly delighted and satisfied with her experience. But God had placed within her heart a desire for something more, and she said, 'I don't want to go down until the power of the Holy Spirit puts me down.' There was a witness in my spirit that it was right for her to take that attitude.

On the Sunday morning before I went to the meeting I found that God was preparing me very deeply; it was like waves of power rolling over my spirit, and I knew that He was going to do a mighty work in that life and that she was going to go down under His power. During the Sunday morning service, when the atmosphere got suitably rich, I called her out for prayer. As she began to go through into the presence of God there came phenomenal power on us. It was so intense that I had a job to remain on my feet; I began to wonder if I would be down before my friend – which in some ways, I suppose, would have been quite amusing! And yet I do not want to make light of that wonderful, wonderful power.

As we prayed I saw fire come down upon her. Seeing fire touch her, my natural thought was, 'Oh, surely she'll go down now.' And, you know, she didn't. I could feel waves of power coming over her, and I could feel that she was fighting it: like Pauline, not rebelling against God, but determined to remain on her feet until the power of the Holy Ghost put her down. I watched that life and saw it as a sacrifice on the altar. It was as though she was standing on the altar, and the fire came down and intensified in and around her until I knew in my spirit that the point would come when she would be totally consumed, and at that point she would drop to the floor. And it happened just as I saw it in my spirit. I saw the fire come down intensely, I saw the moment she was totally taken by God, and I saw her go down under the power of the Spirit. And (again like Pauline) she just crumpled in a heap, neither forwards nor backwards; she just went down.

Staggering to the nearest chair I sat down, feeling (like Pauline again) dazed by the power of the Holy Ghost, as though my physical body was stunned by the power that I had experienced. The person who came out as a 'catcher' also had exactly the same feeling of being dazed by a tremendous power and hardly able to remain upright. I continued taking the rest of the meeting, but couldn't sit in my chair. God was so big, and so holy, and so pure, that I had to kneel in His presence. Then even kneeling wasn't enough, and I had to go down low on the floor just to be in that atmosphere and in that presence. It was a wonderful meeting; access to God was very easy, and we were through in the glory. All through that afternoon I found a great power on myself. It just didn't lift. It was as if something had come to stay (I didn't want it to go away), and I was abiding in this deep, deep atmosphere of God.

I came to the night meeting with an enormous sense

of anticipation. I actually felt as I used to do when I was younger and would come to meetings feeling quite sick with excitement! There was such a sense that God was going to do something wonderful. The anointing was so deep I wondered if I would be able to cope with the first part of the meeting. And, you know, God was gracious, and He lifted the anointing a little for the beginning of the service. Not that I would have any objections to going in at that depth from the very beginning, but others present might have needed more preparation to cope with it.

After preaching I made an appeal, and about ten people came out for ministry. When I went to the first, a girl of twelve or thirteen, though knowing God would meet her I did not, to be honest, expect to feel the power that I felt when praying with her. It was after leaving her and going to the second person that I noticed I had actually staggered; the power was so intense at that point that I could hardly remain on my feet. The second was a young person who has been out several times for ministry, and again I did not expect to feel such a depth of the power of God. She stayed on her feet a little longer than she had done before, and I think probably caught more of the power of God that was in the anointing. She too went down, and I must have been going quite far out of the body myself, because without noticing it I apparently staggered again and found myself leaning against the wall to get my bearings. The power did not continue at that level with everyone; I suppose lives were open at different levels. But with some there came wave upon wave until I really began to feel I was almost holding God out to stay on my feet. I was keeping something extremely tightly shut to stay upright. But I knew that I was to minister – that God had sent me for that purpose – and that wasn't a problem.

For the first time that I have ever done so, I felt I should give a second invitation. A lady came out whom I was very pleased about; she had not been long converted. The look on her face was one of, 'I'm not too sure about this, but I'll just come out anyway.' A very spiritual person, she turned Godward and to her horror she began to fall immediately. You could actually see the consternation passing over her face as she realized she was going down: 'Oh, what's happening to me?' After about five minutes she began to get back up, and I felt to go to her again. Again she went down – and stayed down for a long time.

And now events took a personal turn:

I wanted to be careful. When God's glory comes in I can forget everybody and everything and just go out and enjoy myself. Knowing that God had given responsibility as well, I wanted to make sure that the time was right. I was not conscious at the time of what I did next, but afterwards, looking back, I realized I had done it. In my head I went down the two roads; I saw the left-hand road was the road of staying at that level, of holding the power out and going home like that. And I felt terribly unsatisfied, as if something wouldn't be complete. I turned down the other road to opening up and letting that power flood in. Ministry was finished, the meeting was going on well, and I felt the Spirit wanted me to do that.

I asked someone to take the meeting for me, saying, 'I'm going for ministry.'

'You're what?'

'I'm going for ministry. Just you get on with the meeting. No looking!'

To someone else I said, 'Would you pray with me, please?'

'What?'

'Just pray with me. Don't ask any questions – talk later.'

Moving to a space on the floor, I was beginning to

close my eyes and go out when my friend said to me,
'You'll need to move further forward, you know!'

Immediately there was the self-conscious feeling,
'Oh, dear, I've done what everybody else does when
they don't leave themselves enough space!' I binned
that, and just turned Godward, and I opened that bit
inside that had had to remain shut to keep the full
tide of power out while I led the meeting.

And I went totally unconscious. I don't remember
what happened. I don't remember falling, or landing
on the floor, or whether I was helped down. I don't
know if I crashed down. I don't know what happened.

Diana recovered consciousness in stages:

I was not aware of my body to start with. I became
aware, if you like, first of the unconscious part of me,
then the subconscious part, then the conscious part,
and finally my physical being. (I did not analyse it like
that at the time.) Just as I woke up, or came to, I
became aware of the deeps of my being. The very
deepest parts of my spiritual life were filled with the
ocean of God, were absolutely filled with the life and
power and vitality of God. I can't put it into any
other words than those. I felt absolutely full. And
whereas I had felt wearied and stressed out the week
before, in less than the twinkling of an eye God had
come and filled my whole being.

I had one arm across my middle, and couldn't even
keep it there. It was as though there was an immense
weight, and I just had to allow my whole being to go
right down under the anointing of God. It was sheer
relief to give way to that power: sheer relief not to
walk about staggering, trying to hold it out and
remain upright, but just to give way and let God
enter in the glory of His power. I did not stay down a
long time; feeling that in some ways the work had
been done, I rose to continue with the meeting.

I have found an enormous change since then. For two days afterwards I was scarcely in the body. Every time my mind, body and spirit were free I felt as though I was going out into another dimension. I seemed hardly in this world. I had had that experience before when God met me unusually deeply one night, after which I felt as though I drifted in and out the body for five days. And it was the same again. There was a tremendous unction of the Holy Spirit. I felt physically different and more alive than I have felt for a long time. Some of my friends tell me that when I am under assault I look old. I wish they could have seen me last week at the young people's meeting! I felt younger than the young people! I felt vibrantly alive and full of the joy and the power of God. Since then I have found wonderful access into His presence.

Even now I am aware of that deep, awesome presence and power of God, aware of tuning into something that is not influenced by human unction but is purely divine, aware of coming in at that level to the glory of the Lord God of Hosts. I believe one of the things that has come through this new ministry is that we have tuned into God. We have come through Christ to the Father. He has brought us to Jehovah. And I feel that more and more of the church are meeting with the living God.

Diana's concluding observation was particularly relevant to our own congregation, but could be helpful in principle for others as well. Less than four years before the beginning of the new ministry, Elizabeth H. Taylor, the spiritual mother of the Struthers movement, had passed away.[2] It was inevitable that some of those who valued her ministry should wonder, 'What would Miss Taylor think? This is so different from the olden days.' Diana remarked:

Though I didn't know Miss Taylor particularly well at a personal level, I knew her spiritually and had the

114

privilege of often being brought under her ministry. And I have often been aware of the anointing that was on her being on myself in the deliverance ministry – Grace Gault [3] and I have both been aware of that at times. It is almost as though she is close, and yet it is not she herself but the anointing that was on her, and the feeling of that same power and unction pouring through oneself.

And in the new ministry I have been acutely aware of tuning into an anointing that she carried, of a presence of God that was awesome and dynamic and brought the knowledge of the Lord God of Hosts. I thank God that it is our privilege as the church of Christ that more and more of us should move into that anointing.

The anointing of the holy – not an external form of service, old or new – was the key to the continuing life of God with us as a movement.

In circumstances such as these was it any wonder that we were frequently reminded of such scriptures as those describing the coming of the glory of the Lord upon the newly dedicated temple of Solomon, so that *'the priests could not perform their service'* [4] – or, as an older translation has it, *'the priests could not stand to minister'*?

Notes

[1] Pauline Anderson's unusual experience of the new ministry is featured in *A View from the Floor*, chapter 8. A subsequent experience which helped to explain the first is described in the third book of the series.

[2] Elizabeth H. Taylor's life story is told in Part 2 of my book *A Trumpet Call to Women* (New Dawn Books, 1988). See also *E.H. Taylor: A Modern Christian Mystic: Sayings and Recollections* (New Dawn Books, 1994).

[3] My daughter Grace Gault, who has the care of our Greenock church, appears in the third book of this series. She has contributed material to my *Revival: Living in the Realities* (New Dawn Books, 1993) and *War in Heaven and Earth* (New Wine Press, 1996).

[4] 1 Kings 8:11 (NIV – followed by AV). Cf. 2 Chronicles 7:2.

Note to Readers

If you would like to enquire further about issues raised in this book or if you feel that the compiler could be of help, you are invited to write to him at 27 Denholm Street, Greenock, PA16 8RH, Scotland, or telephone 01475-729668 or 01475-787432.

It may also be of interest to know that Hugh Black is normally involved in five conferences in Scotland each year – New Year, Easter, July, August and October. Friends gather from many parts of Britain. An open invitation is extended to all and particularly to those interested in the baptism in the Holy Spirit and related themes. Details will be provided on enquiry (tel. 0141-339-3543).

Other Books by Hugh Black

The Baptism in the Spirit and Its Effects   **£4.99**

Used in bringing people into the baptism in the Spirit and described as one of the clearest, most incisive books on the subject. This expanded edition includes evidence that Finney, Moody and Spurgeon spoke in tongues, and narrates miraculous effects of the baptism in the lives of Jimmy Lunan and Allan Wiggins.

Reflections on the Gifts of the Spirit   **£2.75**

Deals in an original way with its subject. The chapters on miracles, healings and discernment (with exorcism) have roused great interest and led to positive action. Anecdotes and illustrations have been much appreciated.

Reflections on a Song of Love   **£1.25**

A highly original commentary on 1 Corinthians 13. The drawing power of love pervades this fascinating study. The author shows very clearly how this chapter fully supports and in no way detracts from the doctrine of Pentecost.

A Trumpet Call to Women   £2.50

Presents a strong case from Scripture for greater involvement of women in ministry. It throws much light on those portions which on the surface seem to put women in a subject role. It includes the testimony of Elizabeth H. Taylor, a lady much used of God. A stirring book, demanding a response – a call to action.

Consider Him   £2.25

Considers a number of the qualities of Christ. He Himself seems to speak from the pages of the book, both in the main text and in the testimony of Jennifer Jack, whose selfless presentation truly leaves the reader to consider Christ.

Battle for the Body   £2.95

It will take courage to face the truths highlighted in this original approach to fundamental issues of sanctification. The second part presents the powerful testimony of John Hamilton – a preacher widely known and loved.

The Clash of Tongues: With Glimpses of Revival   £2.75

Part One is a commentary on 1 Corinthians 14. It deals in detail with some of the more difficult questions. Part Two deals with the relationship between revival and Pentecost and refers to the 1939 and 1949 revivals in Lewis, introducing a number of people who were involved in the first of these – particularly Mary MacLean, whose remarkable testimony is related. This book may particularly appeal to people studiously inclined.

The Incomparable Christ   £2.75

Part One deals with the gospel. It faces honestly the questions of Christ's resurrection and that of all men.

It deals in a direct way with the doctrine of hell and eternal judgment, and gives practical instruction on the way of salvation. Part Two presents the remarkable testimonies of two young ladies.

Gospel Vignettes £2.95

Focuses attention on various facets of the gospel, with chapter titles like: Ye Must Be Born Again, The Life-Giving Water, Weighed in the Balances, Behold I Stand at the Door and Knock, The Hour of Decision. Includes testimonies of three people whose lives have been transformed by Christ, to one of whom Christ Himself appeared. Useful in the gospel, but introducing the Pentecostal dimension.

Reflections from Abraham £2.50

Outlines spiritual principles seen in the life of Abraham. It deals with his call and ours, the mountain as distinct from the valley life, intercession, Lot in Sodom, the sacrifice of Isaac and the way of faith. Part Two tells of the action of God in the life of Dorothy Jennings, to whom Abraham has been of particular significance.

Reflections from Moses:
With the Testimony of Dan McVicar £2.99

Part One shows the outworking of spiritual principles such as the calling and training of a man of God, the need to start from holy ground, deliverance from bondage, and the consequences of Moses' failure in a critical hour. Part Two presents the well-known evangelist Dan McVicar's story in his own words. The conversion of this militant communist and the intervention of God in the lives of his parents make thrilling reading.

Christb the Deliverer   £2.99

Deals with both physical and spiritual deliverance. It includes a number of remarkable testimonies to healing, e.g. from blindness, manic depression, ME, rheumatoid arthritis, spinal injury, phobias, nightmares. It speaks of the appearance of angels, touches on revival and analyses the theory of 'visualization'.

Christian Fundamentals   £3.50

Part One deals with the individual and his needs in the realms of Salvation, Baptism in the Spirit, and Deliverance. Part Two focuses on the outflow of the life of God to meet the needs of others through Vocal, Hidden and Open Power Ministries. The End Times are the subject of Part Three.

Reflections from David   £3.75

This searching book shows a man after God's own heart in the glory of his achievements and the tragedy of his failings. Divine retribution and forgiveness, the joy of deliverance, and the action of God in present-day lives are all examined.

Pioneers of the Spiritual Way   £4.99

From a lost Eden our race walked a lost road, occasionally experiencing higher things as pioneers of the spiritual way led upwards. The impassable barrier between God and man was finally removed as the last Adam blasted a way through: Christ, bringing many sons to glory.

Revival:
Including the Prophetic Vision of Jean Darnall   £3.99

Some of the great revivals of the past are reviewed with their enduring principles and changing patterns. Revival comes nearer as we are confronted with more recent movements of God. The celebrated vision of

Jean Darnall has left many with a feeling of keen expectation for coming days.

Revival: Personal Encounters   £4.50

From the treasure chest of memory the author brings a series of revival-related incidents. We hear of Studd, Burton and Salter and of revival in the Congo and Rwanda. More is revealed of the moving of God in Lewis and at an unusual Scottish school camp. A contemporary scene in Brazil brings revival very close. The highly original testimony of Alison Speirs brings the fact and challenge right to our doorstep.

Revival: Living in the Realities   £3.99

For a revived or a revival-conscious people a high level of Christian living is immediately presented. The experience of revival has to be outworked. This book ponders issues such as spiritual warfare, what it means to be imitators of Christ, the need to progress from forgiveness to love for those who do us harm, and the mystery of the love of God itself. An unusual and thought-provoking approach.

E.H. Taylor: A Modern Christian Mystic: Sayings and Recollections   £4.50

A sequel to *Trumpet Call to Women*, this highly unusual book contains insights into a wide range of spiritual themes on the part of one who was much used in predictive prophecy and in leading people into the baptism in the Spirit and deliverance, and especially into a deep knowledge of Christ.

War in Heaven and Earth   £6.99

This book illuminates the subject of spiritual warfare both at the 'ground level' of day-to-day living where the devil's weapons are met with the weapons of Christ, and at the unseen level of conflict where the power of Christ breaks the hold of spiritual entities over specific territorial areas.

A View from the Floor   £5.99

What happens when the power of the Holy Spirit comes upon someone? The first of a series, this book of testimonies traces the effects of a spiritual movement which began in November 1994 and continues to the present time. It is fascinating to learn some of the detail of what happens when we find ourselves on God's operating table.

Book Orders

New Dawn Bookshop, 10A Jamaica Street, Greenock
Renfrewshire, PA15 1YB, Scotland
Telephone 01475 729668   Fax 01475 728145

ORDER FORM

Please send me books by Hugh B. Black indicated below:

Quantity	Title	Price
_____	The Baptism in the Spirit and Its Effects	£4.99
_____	Reflections on the Gifts of the Spirit	£2.75
_____	Reflections on a Song of Love (A commentary on 1 Corinthians 13)	£1.25
_____	A Trumpet Call to Women	£2.50
_____	Consider Him (Twelve Qualities of Christ)	£2.25
_____	Battle for the Body	£2.95
_____	The Clash of Tongues: With Glimpses of Revival	£2.75
_____	The Incomparable Christ	£2.75
_____	Gospel Vignettes	£2.95
_____	Reflections from Abraham	£2.50
_____	Reflections from Moses: With the Testimony of Dan McVicar	£2.99
_____	Christ the Deliverer	£2.99
_____	Christian Fundamentals	£3.50

(cont. overleaf)

_____	Reflections from David	£3.75
_____	Pioneers of the Spiritual Way	£4.99
_____	Revival: Including the Prophetic Vision of Jean Darnall	£3.99
_____	Revival: Personal Encounters	£4.50
_____	Revival: Living in the Realities	£3.99
_____	E.H. Taylor: A Modern Christian Mystic	£4.50
_____	War in Heaven and Earth	£6.99
_____	A View from the Floor	£5.99
_____	Further Views from the Floor	£5.99

Name . . . .

Address . . . .

. . . .

. . . . Post Code . . . .

Please add 50p per book for postage and packing.